Running Mount Rainier

An Ordinary Runner's Journey from Crippling Injury to Ultra Marathon Finish Line

Mark Stone

Running Mount Rainier:

An Ordinary Runner's Journey from Crippling Injury to Ultra Marathon Finish Line

©2021 Mark Stone

Cover Art by Jennevieve Schlemmer (all rights reserved)
ISBN: 9780578303710

TABLE OF CONTENTS

FOREWORD

This journey would not have been possible without the love and support of my whole family; I am particularly grateful to my wife Karen, and my youngest son Nathan. They have been supportive when long training runs have eaten up weekend time. They have attended more races than I ever thought they would. And each of them, in very different ways, has pursued a difficult journey to better health that has been a vital inspiration for me.

And so this work is dedicated to Karen and Nathan.

There are others I wish to thank.

Thanks to all of my backers on Kickstarter, whose funding made the publication of this book possible, including the special backers:

- Vern and Amy Montarbo.
- Mark Griffith;
- Lou Shapiro;
- Bill Chamis;
- Greg Sanders;
- David Stier;
- Clarence and Mary Stone.

I'd like to offer a heartfelt remembrance for William Imle, who passed tragically in 2007. Bill and I had an unusual relationship, he being part friend, part mentor, and part co-conspirator in the kind of shenanigans of which only teenage boys are capable. He gave me confidence in my athleticism at a time in my life when self-confidence was a fragile thing. I miss his unique blend of optimism, impishness, and soulfulness.

I'd like to thank Karyn Lush and Jason Mueller, who offered me counsel and encouragement during the time I worked at Nike.

To Scott Holder: you are in a whole different class of ultra runner, but your consistent encouragement and occasional well-placed piece of advice have mattered a lot over the years.

I'd also like to thank Clay Garrard, my lunchtime running companion during the years we both worked in Disney's Seattle office. Deep friendships are often hard to form later in life, but those runs and the conversations we shared formed the foundation of a friendship that lasts to this day.

And I want to thank the Alexandra, Mike, Eoin, Seth, and the rest of the Etsy Run Club for lots of thoughtful conversation on running, and for introducing me to the joys of running in New York City (and occasionally Dublin).

It takes a village to get a book from final draft to printed copy, so thanks to:

- Melissa Prideaux for her edits; this book is so much better for her contributions large and small.
- Jennevieve Schlemmer for her amazing cover art.
- Ed Healy and the gang at Gamerati for their expertise in Kickstarter fulfillment.
- Lynn Mackey for her layout and design acumen; my words would never have been print-ready otherwise.

Finally, I have the deepest gratitude for my fellow Compulsive Runners and the nurturing, encouraging, and educating community they have provided me over the years. They came along at a unique time in our society, and a unique time in my life, when I really needed just such a group.

Google's release of the first Android phone in 2010 coincided with my decision to return to running. For the first time, GPS technology had become cheap enough and portable enough that it was pervasive in the running world. Pretty much every runner I knew had either a GPS watch, an iPhone, or an Android device.

As marvelous as this brave new digital world sounded at the time, there were lots of growing pains along the way. At first I used Google Maps from my desktop computer to figure out distances of running routes so that I at least knew how far I was running. Then I acquired an early Android phone and started tracking my runs. Early smartphones were not especially waterproof, and in the Pacific Northwest's soggy climate I've lost numerous phones to water damage.

The early mapping software was not very accurate. I switched between running apps regularly during that time, and was both amused and frustrated at the differences. Google Maps on my computer would tell me that a route was 6.0 miles. Endomondo on my phone would track it as 7.1 miles; MapMyRun would track it as 5.7. At one point I supposedly ran a two minute mile. On another run I did an out and back where the out leg recorded as 8 miles and the return leg over the exact same route recorded as 18 miles. Zooming all the way into the waypoint level, the route I had supposedly followed on one of these irregular runs looked like a spider on LSD laying web.

All of these programs are getting smarter. The math gets better at interpolating between sparse data points. Cell phone tower location data, or wifi hotspot data can supplement GPS data when GPS coverage is not good. Watches and phones can now use accelerometer data to estimate distance covered. And like every other piece of chip and radio technology, the hardware continues to get smaller, less expensive, and more accurate.

It's hard to imagine that earlier time when none of these digital tools existed. I have nothing but admiration for the pioneers of trail running who headed off into the wilderness with only a topo map and a compass with which to navigate. I am also a little envious of the freedom they enjoyed, running with no regard for time elapsed or distance covered. In today's tech saturated world it is too easy to obsess over the data presented by our digital selves, and to feel needlessly anxious when we are disconnected from that data.

The other important technology trend that has impacted the running community is the rise of social media, and this brings me back to Compulsive Runners. The Internet makes it possible for people who share a common interest but not necessarily geographical proximity to find and share with each other. Services like Twitter and Facebook make it easy to connect and share, particularly as those services have extended from desktop computing to the mobile world.

For me, social media solved a dilemma. On the one hand, I am a solo runner. Yes, I love the social and festive atmosphere of a big race. And yes, our neighborhood has a local running store where runners gather, and twice a≈week — Saturday mornings and Wednesday evenings — do training runs together. However, I have always preferred the solitude of a long run alone. I find this time meditative, calming, and spiritual. On the other hand, I face the same challenges of motivation, and have the same peer support needs as any other ordinary runner. Through social media I found an online group of runners that both inspired me and held me accountable while at the same time I continued my solitary running.

During the period I focus on here — the 34 months from December 2012 to October 2015 — my social media platform of choice was Google's then nascent and now defunct Google+. I signed up immediately with its launch in summer 2011 and the fellow runners I encountered there were an enormous help. They inspired and motivated me, as well as giving just plain practical advice as I readied for my first marathon in November of 2012. By January of 2013, as I was planning my training for the Winthrop Marathon, I had settled into a nice little group called "Compulsive Runners" on Google+. At our peak there were about 40 of us, which is a good size for an online community. We represented the diversity of the running community — men and women, runners from England, Holland, Germany, Australia, and New Zealand as well as the U.S., and runners at every distance from 10K to ultra marathon.

Quite honestly, it's hard for me to imagine how amateur runners gathered information and formed training and race plans before the Internet. As I transitioned from "I need to start running regularly and get back into shape" into "I need a plan that will get me to an effective 10K / half marathon / marathon for my capabilities", I had many questions:

- How many times a week should I run?
- How do I balance speed work versus distance work?
- How fast should my distance runs be?
- How far should my speed runs be?
- What's the benefit of cross training?
- What should I eat?
- What's a sensible hydration and food strategy in a race?
- How much time do I need to train for a given race distance?
- How do I balance training time and recovery time?
- What is a fartlek?
- What is interval training?
- What is HRM or MAF training?
- What do I do about cramps?
- Tendonitis?
- Runner's knee?
- Does yoga help?
- Foam rolling?
- Kinesiology tape?
- Compression socks?

Thanks to Compulsive Runners, I have found answers to many of these questions, and resources to develop my own theories about the others. I have resolved a number of small injury problems without recourse to a doctor, and I have had medical consultations where I have been the most knowledgeable person in the room.

More importantly, I have found inspiration and companionship from dozens of runners and their stories. Asthmatics; cancer survivors; veterans transitioning to civilian life; atheists; devout Christians; Buddhists — all are ordinary people made extraordinary by the spiritual journey that running has become for them. Through them I have discovered what a humble and welcoming community runners are. They truly understand that we are each on our own journey — no distance is too short, no pace too slow, no goal too modest, and yet no aspiration out of reach. Even the most ordinary of runners can accomplish the extraordinary.

I'd like to give thanks to all who spent time in the Compulsive Runners community, and I'd like to call out a few by name who deserve special mention:

- Kristi Kubota and Dean Colprit, for founding Compulsive Runners.
- Otto Daly, fellow Pacific Northwest trail runner who introduced me to the Primal Endurance approach.
- Mark Berry and Robbi Berry, for their steadfast participation and support in our little group.
- Ken Ludt, because every group needs a bit of a joker and mischief maker to open up unexpected adventures. Ken and I shared what would become one of my most unexpected running adventures.
- Jason Sealy, a person so very different from me and yet a kindred spirit; truly the brother in running I didn't know I could have.
- Michael Mankus — the "Machine" — whose ultra achievements are an inspiration to us all, and whose humble humor has brought us joy and laughter.
- Michele Sun, in many ways the most dedicated and accomplished runner I know, who has prevailed in spite of the daunting obstacles that life has put before her. What started as an online acquaintance has grown into a deep friendship in which we have run together, raced together, and shared meals and conversation that have meant so much to me.

- Tracie Rodriguez, who combined as much passion and talent for distance running as any runner I've met. Her unusual blend of youthful enthusiasm and timeless wisdom helped me along at a critical early time in my growth as a runner.
- Jenny Darrow, truly my mentor in running. Her quiet encouragement and sage advice pre-dates Compulsive Runners. Anchor yourself to the joy of running, and training and discipline will take care of themselves. That is wisdom she has shared in words, and modeled in conduct. I have learned so much from her example.

CHAPTER 1

SEATTLE MARATHON

November 2012 | Seattle

"The true measure of a runner is not completing the race you know you can run; it is completing the race you never knew you could run."

Scheduling a marathon in late November in Seattle is a little crazy, and picking that event for a first marathon is even crazier. The choice made sense at the time. I had finished my second half marathon in May of 2012, and finished well. My goal for that half marathon had been to finish under two hours, and I had finished in 1:56:20. As I pondered new challenges, simply running a faster half marathon didn't seem enough.

Yet to contemplate a full marathon was beyond intimidating. To say that a full marathon is twice the distance of a half, misses the point. That's like noting that Mount Everest is twice the height of Mount Rainier. It doesn't mean that the former is merely twice as hard to climb as the latter; what happens in the second half utterly changes the character of the endeavor. Running a half marathon is no more preparation for a full marathon than a jaunt up Mount Rainier is preparation for tackling Everest.

Still, with some encouragement from my runner friends who were experienced marathoners, and with the cautious support of my wife Karen, I signed up for the Seattle Marathon. I figured I would need a good five months to train, and I made my decision in early June. Thus I found myself looking for a race date deep into the fall. At 15,000 runners, Seattle has the festival atmosphere of a big city marathon, and that was something I wanted to experience.

Race day arrives.

I cross the finish line. Karen is waiting with juice and a jacket, the most welcome sight I've ever seen. We take a few minutes to relax in the Seattle Center Armory so I can be off my feet for the first time in roughly five hours. Now we make our way back to the car, and I sit inside. I'm shivering like crazy. Why am I so cold?

Rewind to 5:15 AM when I wake up.

The forecast is for sunny and cold, with morning fog. At the Space Needle, where the race will start, the expectation is about 40 degrees for the 8:15 start time. This will be my first race in the last three years where it hasn't rained, so I'm pretty happy about that. I figure the morning fog will start to burn off by around 10:00, and I dress accordingly: I wear my felt cap, and I layer two long sleeve shirts, but I stick with shorts and my comfy thin socks.

My hope is for something around 4 hours 15 minutes, but I expect to come in a little bit slower than that. If I'm under 4 hours 30 minutes I'll be happy. At start time I find myself lined up behind the 4:40 pace runner, and in the first half mile I pass her and the 4:25 pace runner. I never see the 4 hour pace runner, and that's fine by me. I'm feeling confident, and settle into a good pace.

After an opening mile or so through downtown Seattle, and a long curve along the I-90 flyway, we drop down to the out and back to Mercer Island along the I-90 floating bridge, followed by an out and back down to Seward Park (a small peninsula sticking out into Lake Washington). The temperature drops. Noticeably. The fog shows no sign of lifting.

Around Mile 6, coming off the bridge, I feel some stiffness in my left hamstring. This is not a new experience. With nerve damage on my right side from a back injury I tend to favor my left leg, and it does tighten up from doing most of the work. Typically it loosens up once I warm up. I've done two

21 mile training runs and two 18 mile training runs with exactly that experience, so I'm not worried.

I cross the halfway point on the backside of Seward Park with a time of 2 hours 4 minutes, which I'm very happy with. I feel I've been holding back, saving strength for the second half. Given the slow first couple of miles as the mob sorted itself out, I'm feeling that a time under 4 hours 15 minutes is a real possibility.

Then at Mile 14, right next to the first aid station, my left hamstring suddenly goes from chronic stiffness to cramp. An immobilizing full cramp. It's a weird feeling when your hopes about finishing time are dashed in an instant. You are now fighting a completely different battle. The only question is "Can I finish?" The first aid tent is right there, tempting me to bow out. And certainly I don't want to risk injury. "Running for a lifetime" matters to me, and no one race is worth risking that. But so far, it feels like a cramp, not an injury. A debilitating cramp to be sure, but just a cramp. So I stretch for a few minutes, and walk for a few minutes. Gingerly, I start to jog. I'm thinking, "Just take it mile by mile."

By Mile 18 the cramp has not let up, but if I keep my stride short I can still manage a slow jog. I cross the 18 Mile mark just under 3 hours. Given the setbacks, I'm pretty happy to still be in the race, and satisfied with my time. Then my energy level just completely collapses. I have hit the proverbial wall, and though I struggle through the remaining eight miles, I never break through. The 4:25 pace runner passes me at Mile 19. The 4:40 pace runner passes me at Mile 23. I jog every downhill over the last eight miles, and much of the flat stretches. The rest I just walk. A brisk walk, but walking nonetheless. From deep in the tunnel vision of my suffering I am aware, and strangely heartened, to note that I am surrounded by other "walking wounded" down the stretch.

One other discovery down the stretch. Normally I'm very anti-sports drink. The whole industry strikes me as a big opportunity for charlatanism.

So typically I stick to water; the notion that there's a fueling strategy to be figured out for endurance running has not yet occurred to me. By about Mile 22 I feel that water is just not getting the job done. I'm completely spent. So I take a chance on Gatorade at the next station, and my body immediately cries, "Yes! More of that!" I hit every station from there to the finish, and reach strictly for Gatorade. It gets me through, giving me something to think about for future races.

And so here I am, post race, shivering uncontrollably in the front seat of the car.

I realize several things, kind of all at once. First, I am borderline hypothermic. Second, the fog didn't really burn off until well after noon. Third, the temperature along Lake Washington (miles 4 — 19) was probably in the mid-30s, and I am in no way dressed for that. Finally, the energy drain I felt by Mile 18 was probably due to my body having expended too much energy at that point just trying to keep me warm. I had done four training runs of equal or greater length and suffered no such energy drain. Yes, I had the muscle cramp, but honestly all my muscles in both legs just felt tight from about Mile 13 on. And the cramp, while certainly related to the asymmetry in my gait, was also significantly aggravated by the fact that my legs just never did completely warm up.

I didn't respect the weather conditions. And I paid the price. But two thoughts kept running through my head down the stretch: "I never want to experience this again" and "I definitely don't want to experience this and not finish." And of course the thought that finally tipped the balance for me: "Everything that my wife tries to do with her health is far harder than what I'm doing. I don't expect her to give up, so I can't give up either because that might make her weaker."

Head games. We runners play them all the time.

So what have I learned? Being a runner and being a marathoner are not the same thing. However comfortable, however at peace I am with running, the marathon — both training and execution — is still an enigma to me.

Yet I have learned how far I can push myself and not quit. And I have learned what drives me on when all else fails. Karen and I are very different people with very different challenges, but an essential part of our love is the way, oft unspoken, that we inspire each other.

I had thought that completing the Seattle Marathon would be the end of a journey. Instead it proved to be only the next chapter in my journey as a runner, and only the very beginning of my journey as a marathoner.

CHAPTER 2

YOU CAN'T SAY WE NEVER TRIED

June 1998 | Menlo Park, California

We sat on the same couch, but not close to each other, each silent for the moment, staring straight ahead.

We had met 15 years earlier, I as a new graduate student at the University of Rochester, and she as an undergraduate. A refugee from the Soviet Union, she was beautiful, exotic, and caught the eye of every young man at the school.

I grew up in an academic household. My parents met as graduate students at Duke University, and my dad ultimately settled into a tenured position as professor of political science at the University of Maryland. As a kid, when people used to ask me what I wanted to be when I grew up, I always interpreted that to mean what department did I want to be a professor in. My parents made sure that my sister and I spent time at the Smithsonian museums, the National Gallery, and regularly attended events at the Kennedy Center. We were assured not just a good education, but a cultured life experience.

So when I met this enchanting Eastern European woman, I thought I had found everything I was supposed to be looking for — someone also cultured and academic, someone who would be an intellectual partner, who would challenge me to broaden my horizons with experiences from a different world. Someone with whom I could form a relationship akin to the one my parents had.

There was just one problem. She didn't want to be in the United States.

It was her father's decision to leave the Soviet Union, a decision he made under complicated personal circumstances, without consulting the rest of the family. The Soviet Union was a signatory to the 1974 Helsinki Accord, providing a path for emigration. That path was not short and the outcome uncertain. Anyone wishing to emigrate was considered disloyal to the Communist Party. Her mother and father both lost their jobs. She was expelled from Moscow State University in a humiliating ceremony in front of the entire student body.

For two years they waited. At last permission came, and the family made their way first to Vienna, then to Rome, then to a sponsoring family in Massachusetts, and finally to Rochester where her father had secured a job with Kodak. She left behind her high school and college sweetheart — the love of her life — and a year and a half of study at one of the country's most prestigious universities. Rochester, New York was the last place in the world she wanted to be.

I am a sucker for lost causes. For seven years I helped her find hope when she felt none. I helped her navigate her way to a bachelor's degree through the SUNY system when her parents could no longer afford to pay University of Rochester tuition. I helped her figure out how to apply to graduate school, and followed her to UC Berkeley where she would study under eventual Nobel Laureate Daniel Kahneman. Yet so often the ways I tried to help were not the ways she needed help. She was frustrated by my inability to connect with what she really needed. I was frustrated by what I perceived as a lack of appreciation, and over time frustration festered into resentment. A well-intentioned "white knight" does not necessarily make a good husband.

In 1989 the Berlin Wall came down, and a life she had been torn away from began to open up for her once again. Part of me had always felt like her second choice, and while I felt some resentment over that, I was safe in the knowledge that her first choice wasn't available. The end of the Cold War changed all that.

I met the old boyfriend when he was able to visit Washington, D.C. in 1991. How could I not be happy for her? She was reconnecting face to face with someone she thought she'd never see again. I knew how important it was to her. Yet I felt I was standing on unstable ground. The whole situation felt like a soldier coming home who had been presumed dead. Their old life was gone, but not so all the old feelings.

In 1993 she and I had a son, and for a while that seemed to put us back on solid ground. We had a common purpose in something very important to both of us. We had new friendships with the other parents we came to know. And we had proud grandparents thrilled with this new family we were at last forming. What I didn't understand was how much she worked at keeping our marriage together out of fear — fear of disappointing her father.

In 1996 her father passed away suddenly, and it was like an emotional dam within her finally broke. What had previously been passive-aggressive expressions of displeasure became frank and candid statements of unhappiness. I actually felt relieved; at least we were putting it out in the open. The following summer she announced that she was going to take a trip back to Moscow to visit family. I supported her decision. It felt right, like something she needed to do.

And so here we were, sitting on the couch upon her return. She had visited cousins and aunts she thought she'd never see again. She'd seen the turmoil of post Cold War Russia and found it unappealing. She had reconnected — intimately — with the old boyfriend.

Silence hung in the air for a moment, and then she smiled. "It's a small thing," she said, "but I remember you catching the train that morning."

I knew the event she was talking about. We'd lived in the East Bay at the time, and every weekday morning we'd drive across the Dumbarton Bridge to drop me at the Menlo Park train station so I could commute to my job in San Francisco, and then she'd drop our son at daycare and continue on to her postdoc at NASA Ames Research Center. There was one express train that stopped in Menlo Park each morning and went nonstop to San Francisco. If I missed that train, then I would be late to work. Not just a little late. An hour late. This gauntlet was so difficult to run that we finally decided to move across the Bay to Menlo Park.

On the morning she was referencing, the traffic had been horrendous. The freeways were totally clogged, and I used the neighborhood surface streets to get as close to the Dumbarton Bridge as possible before getting on the highway. Once we crept across the bridge to the other side, the traffic continued to plague us. I tried one back route through Menlo Park to no avail, and then another which was a little better. Time was running out; I didn't see any way to get to the station in time. About 200 yards from the station, traffic came to a complete halt because the road crossed the tracks and the train — the one I was trying to catch — was rolling into the station so the crossing gates were down.

I turned to her in the passenger's seat and said, "You need to drive," then I threw open the car door and sprinted for the train, leaving her to sort it out in the middle of traffic.

"I can't believe you caught that train," she said. "I would have given up so many times that morning."

I chuckled, and replied, "It's not in my nature. But yes, that was a little crazy."

Softly, she said, "You don't know when to give up. It's the thing I love about you." She paused, and her voice hardened, "It's also the thing I hate about you."

We went silent again for a bit. I choked up as I tried to get the words out. "It's over, isn't it?"

She nodded. "Yes. It's over."

CHAPTER 3

LIFT MY EYES UP TO THE HILLS

December 2012 | Buckley, Washington

A big city marathon offers the excitement of the crowd, and the energy from thousands and thousands of other runners. While I was happy to have experienced that atmosphere once, I had no desire to repeat it. In training I am a solitary runner, and part of the appeal of running has always been to have that block of time in communion with nature. So, for my second marathon I wanted something of that communal experience. December found me considering my options.

East of Seattle, across the Cascades, the State of Washington takes on a whole different character. No longer wet and coastal, the land becomes arid and rugged. Grassy rolling hills that are golden brown all summer long mix with pine-covered mountains. The whole region is cut through with steep canyons formed by the many rivers that criss-cross the countryside. Several races on this side of the mountains are organized by Rainshadow Running, a wonderful organization I was only just getting to know. As I looked through their calendar for 2013, one race stood out — the Winthrop Marathon.

Winthrop is a small resort town tucked up against North Cascades National Park, way up by the Canadian border. Dressed up with a frontier theme, in the winter it is home to cross country and downhill skiers. In the summer it's a playground for cyclists, hikers, and fly fishers.

The Winthrop Marathon is small, typically with about 300 runners. The course is unique. From Winthrop, runners travel more than an hour by bus deep into the Okanogan National Forest, and are dropped off where the pavement ends, and the backpacking trails start. From there they run back into town.

I also had my eye on another event, tantalizing in its own way: the 50 mile long Rainier to Ruston Relay.

I live in the Carbon River Corridor, where the Carbon River passes by the towns of Carbonado, Wilkeson, Burnett, Buckley, and South Prairie. This area was mostly settled at the close of the 19th century, with logging and coal mining as the main economic activities. Both required rail lines to get their product to market. The coal mines have long since been tapped out, and lumber moves primarily by truck today. Yet the rail beds remain. Pierce County benefits from the hard work of the non-profit Foothills Rails to Trails Coalition. This group has worked for years to secure the property, or easement rights, and do the work to create a system of paved hiking and biking trails known as the Foothills Trail. In its full vision the Foothills Trail would extend all the way from Mount Rainier National Park to the shores of Puget Sound.

The work of the Coalition is expensive and time consuming. Their biggest source of funding comes from a race that they put on each June. The Rainier to Ruston Relay consists of twelve stages, starting at the Carbon River entrance to Mount Rainier National Park, and finishing on the Commencement Bay waterfront in Tacoma. The 50 mile race is mostly run by teams, typically of three, four, or six runners, who alternate running the twelve stages. Close to 2000 runners undertake this endeavor each year. There are some short sections where runners have to run roadside because no trail yet exists in that area. The upper segments involve a lot of dirt trail, often very technical single track trail running, where the trail exists but cannot feasibly be paved. The lower segments follow the paved portion of the Foothills Trail all the way to Commencement Bay.

The Foothills Trail passes within a mile and a half of my house, and over the years I have run thousands of training miles on it. So I'm a strong believer in the work of the Coalition, and knew I wanted to make a habit of supporting them. At some point I would wanted to assemble a relay team to run the race. But as a first experience I wanted to serve as a volunteer and get a sense first hand of what the race was like.

I made that commitment; June 1 of 2013 I would volunteer with the Rainier to Ruston Relay. The Winthrop Marathon was the following weekend on June 9. I registered; Winthrop would be my second marathon.

No sooner had I registered than I began to ponder how to adjust my training. Part of the attraction of Winthrop was the net elevation drop. Since the race starts up in the mountains and finishes back in town, runners descend a net of 1300 feet over the course. At first glance that seems easier than running a relatively flat course. However, downhill running takes its own toll on the knees and quads, and the starting elevation above 3000 feet gave me pause. While not as challenging as the courses in the 5000 to 7000 range so common in the Rockies, it was enough to make me wonder if I would benefit from some altitude acclimation.

I concluded that running my usual flat, lowland stretch along the Foothills Trail between South Prairie and Orting would not be enough. I needed to incorporate some new terrain into my training. But where to run?

I'll admit that up to this point I had been relatively spoiled as a runner. Living in a rural part of Washington State it was easy to just step out the front door and have a wealth of running routes to choose from. The notion of driving somewhere to a trailhead, as most runners do, had never occurred to me. Yet a 40 minutes drive from my house puts one inside the boundaries of Mount Rainier National Park.

Suddenly it seemed obvious that I should be running on Mount Rainier. Why had I never looked up and thought of this before? As winter turned to spring, the only one question remained: when would the snow line recede far enough to make the mountain accessible?

CHAPTER 4

A WOMAN'S MARATHON

August 1984 | Rochester, New York

That Sunday promised to be another hot August day, and I came downstairs intent on running errands in the relative cool of the morning. Remembering that the Olympics were on, I paused to turn on the TV. I saw women gathering at the track in the Los Angeles Coliseum. Right. The marathon. The first ever Olympic women's marathon. Fidgeting with my car keys, I thought, "Well, I'll just watch the start."

The broadcasters focused on Greta Waitz, who was in the midst of a decade of dominance in the New York City Marathon. I knew the top American runner was Joan Benoit, but didn't really know anything about her. The women all looked so happy — smiling, laughing, relaxed. And why shouldn't they be? On this day they would collectively knock down another barrier to gender equality.

I picked out Joan Benoit, smiling and chatting easily with other runners. Then, just a few minutes before the start, I saw her step away, turn her back to the group, and gather herself. She turned around, shoulders straight, smile gone, her face now a mask of determination. They all stepped to the starting line. With a shot of the starting gun they were off.

The opening few miles had a pack of the top runners jostling for position, with Joan Benoit, Greta Waitz, and Rosa Mota all near the front. They approached the first water station, and I glanced at the front door, thinking of my errands. Then, as the other runners angled to grab a cup of water, Joan Benoit surged, skipping past the water station and separating herself from the pack.

Years later, Joan — now Joan Benoit Samuelson — would say, "I wasn't running my own race. I was in a pack of runners, and my stride was compromised. I wasn't running very efficiently, and I said to myself I need to get out of this pack and run my own race."

I watched, mesmerized. This was very early in the race to be making a move. Usually a break from the pack happens around Mile 18 to 20. Could she keep this up? Putting my car keys away, I sat on the couch, all thought of errands banished.

For the next two hours I watched what should have been the most boring athletic event ever — one woman, running all alone on the streets of Los Angeles. Yet I was completely captivated. She kept her mask of determination, and her strides seemed to just flow over the ground. I am always amazed at how effortless world class marathoners make running look. Joan Benoit was running at a pace of 5:53 per mile. On my best day as a young runner, I could maintain that pace for three miles.

Joan Benoit set three challenges. First, she challenged herself to be in control, to run within herself, and to not need the gauge of other runners' progress to inform her how she was doing. Second, she challenged the other runners with her bold, early move. If any of them made a move to catch her that early, they risked flaming out before the finish. Yet if they waited for the moment when she started to tire, that moment might never come. Finally, she challenged the bright Southern California sun. The ideal temperature for running a marathon is between 48 and 60 degrees. On this day, in a setting reminiscent of Alberto Salazar's and Dick Beardsley's Boston Marathon "Duel in the Sun" from just two years earlier, the temperatures in Los Angeles reached a daunting 86 degrees. For one runner — Gaby Andersen-Schiess — the heat was almost disastrous. She entered the Coliseum for the final lap clearly suffering from heat exhaustion, requiring 5 and a half minutes to stagger around the track to the finish line.

Joan Benoit mastered all three challenges. As she entered the Coliseum to a standing ovation from a capacity crowd, the mask of determination dropped at last, and a radiant smile lit her face. She accelerated the relentless pace she had maintained, appearing to sprint around the final lap to a joyous, raucous finish — a gold medal for herself and America, and a victory for women everywhere.

CHAPTER 5

MOUNT RAINIER

March 2013 | Mount Rainier National Park

Visually, Mount Rainier is one of the most impressive mountains in the world. At 14,409 feet, Rainier's elevation seems unremarkable among the dozens of North American peaks that exceed 14,000 feet. Yet it is one of only two peaks above 14,0000 feet in the lower 48 states (Mount Shasta is the other) that is not connected to either the Sierra Nevada or Rocky Mountain ranges. In other words, it stands higher above its surroundings than many taller peaks do above theirs.

To put that in perspective — base camp at Everest is 18,000 feet, and Everest is just over 29,000 feet. This means that 11,000 feet of mountain rises above the surrounding ridgeline. In the Cascades the ridgeline runs at about 5000 feet, meaning that Rainier soars 9,000 feet above its surroundings. Not quite as massive as Everest, but comparable.

Everyone in the greater Seattle area is aware of how Rainier dominates the skyline. You descend past it on the landing approach to Seatac Airport. You see it from the Space Needle. You see it from the ferries, and from the Tacoma waterfront. Even in the Portland area, almost 200 miles away, there are spots on the west side where you can see Mount Rainier, Mount Saint Helens, and Mount Hood all in the same vista. When you live — as I do — in East Pierce County, Rainier is a giant whose presence can be felt even when obscured by clouds.

Mount Rainier National Park has two main approaches. Coming from the Portland area to the south you follow U.S. Highway 12 up to the Paradise visitor center. Coming from the Seattle area to the North you follow State Route 410 up to the Sunrise visitor center. These two visitors centers receive over one million visitors per year.

Several less traveled routes will also take you into the park. The north face of Mount Rainier is dominated by Carbon Glacier, the largest U.S. glacier outside of Alaska, and the water source for the Carbon River. Just over the western spur of Mount Rainier that forms the beginning of the Carbon River valley is an alpine col at about 6,000 feet elevation. Nestled in the base of this col is Mowich Lake. The drive from my house to Mowich Lake is about an hour. Weather permitting.

At 46.8 degrees north latitude, Mount Rainier is more than halfway from the Equator to the Arctic Circle. It is farther north than Montreal, Quebec City, and Bangor Maine. Snow, and thus glaciers cover it year round. The snow level can reach as low as 2,000 feet in the winter, and generally falls between 7,000 and 9,000 feet during the late summer. Carbon Glacier's base, benefiting from the shade of the north slope, is at 3,500 feet. The peak time of year for wildflowers blooming on Mount Rainier is not springtime. The mountain's gorgeous alpine meadows, where these flowers bloom, are still snowbound until early summer, making August and September the best months to see them.

The difficulty with running a marathon with 1500 feet of elevation drop is that you have to do some training that incorporates a big elevation drop. And the difficulty with training runs that involve big elevation drops is that you have to have equivalent elevation gain in the run. From the town of Carbonado to Mowich Lake the slopes of Mount Rainier gain 4000 feet in elevation. Once I realized I could look past my own front door for running routes, I knew I would spend significant training time along sections of that stretch.

In March I took our son Nathan — he was seven at the time — for a snow day up on the approach to Mowich Lake. We made a snowman, threw snowballs at each other, did some sledding on the saucer. I realized it would be weeks yet before I could use this stretch as a training ground.

So for the time being I kept my running focused on lower elevation. The Saint Paddy's Day run in Tacoma would be my third half marathon. It's a beautiful course. The city of Tacoma has made a real effort to preserve the waterfront with green space along Ruston Way, and the view from Ruston Way out over the water is serene. I truly prefer Tacoma's waterfront over the carnival atmosphere tourist traps of either the Seattle waterfront or San Francisco's Fisherman's Wharf. Ruston Way is predominantly park land and a trail. The horizon is dominated by the green of Vashon Island, and you can see the ferry quietly plying the waters between Vashon Island and Point Defiance.

I finished in 1:57:02, 42 seconds off my PR pace, and I was thrilled with that time. To be at that level of performance this early in the year was a real confidence boost as I looked ahead to the Winthrop Marathon in June. My wife and I finished the morning with lunch at the pub. A frosty, cold New Castle Nut Brown Ale and a plate of bangers and mash really hit the spot after the race, and there's just something very uplifting about a raucous crowd of runners in the Saint Patrick's Day spirit after a really fun run. Leprechaun hats and lime green tutus abounded. Even a kilt or two. And fortune really smiled. By the time we finished lunch it was raining. By the time we drove back home it was pouring. Ah, but for a few precious hours that morning the sun shone, fortune smiled, and the luck of the Irish was with us.

On the last day of March I woke up before dawn, donned my running gear, and ate a quick breakfast in the quiet of the house while everyone else, cats included, still slept. The weather had been good the last few days, and as I stepped out the door it looked like the clear skies would hold. Easing the car out of the driveway I could see the gray dawn light seeping into the sky as I turned towards the town of Wilkeson, a five mile drive from my house.

As I drove towards Wilkeson, the Cascades were silhouetted on the horizon. Like a somber giant Rainier rose, head and shoulders above the rest.

Wilkeson is small, with a population less than 500. It has a bar, a restaurant, a church, and even boasted a distillery for a while. It also has the last gas station. Beyond Wilkeson the road takes a steep upward turn, making the town the unofficial boundary between the region surrounding the White River known as the Plateau, and Mount Rainier itself.

Carbonado is the last town. Another couple of miles and the road crosses the Carbon River on a one lane bridge more than 100 feet above. The area around the bridge is now known as Fairfax, and was once the site of two company towns, Fairfax and Melmont, built and operated by the Northern Pacific Railroad, which also owned the coal mine in the area. In the Sixties the land was auctioned off, and today there are a handful of residents in the area who took advantage of the bargain auction prices. This area is incredibly remote, and the folks who live here are reclusive by nature; some commune-aspiring hippies still living in a Sixties mindset, some survivalist libertarians found in remote pockets throughout Oregon, Washington, Idaho, and Montana.

By the time I left Carbonado the sky was turning blue, and while temperatures were still in the 40s the day promised to be bright and warm. Where was the snow line? I really had no idea, never having driven the Mowich Lake approach this time of year. Erring on the side of caution I opted to park near the bottom, just a couple of miles past the Fairfax Bridge at an elevation of about 1500 feet. Stepping out of the car I took in the view while I waited for my phone to pick up a GPS lock so I could track my run.

Across the road the ridge fell away into the Carbon River valley. Carbon Glacier itself lay out of sight behind the next pine-covered ridge across that valley. Mist still hid the basin, but above the head of the valley Rainier's snow cap rose, clear and sparkling. Above me, the road continued and quickly disappeared into forest. I felt a moment of trepidation as my abstract training plan gave way to the immediacy of the climb before me. I had a 12 mile run planned for the day, and so the first six miles would be all uphill at an average grade of about 5%. A quick glance showed that my phone was ready. I set off.

One hard lesson for every runner is that you cannot run a long run too slowly. Building stamina with the weekly long run is a completely separate activity from building speed and strength with shorter, faster runs. Push too hard on your long run and you wear yourself down more than you build yourself up. I had finally begun to appreciate this lesson, and as I slowly jogged up the road I kept reminding myself to take whatever walking breaks I needed as the climb began to wear on me.

Yes, the running was hard. But the setting was energizing. At Mile 2 I turned around and could see the lower slopes of Mount Rainier falling away below me to the Plateau, the towns of Buckley and Enumclaw lost in the ripples and furrows of the hills. At Mile 4 the snowcap of Rainier looked so close I felt like I could reach out and touch it.

After Mile 4 the road reaches the crest of the ridgeline and crosses over. For the first time I could see all the way to the western horizon. Midway to the horizon I could see the glimmer of the skyscrapers in downtown Tacoma, and barely make out the hazy blue smudge that was the southern reach of Puget Sound beyond. Way out on the western horizon I could just make out an undulating line of white that at first I took for clouds. Looking closer, and waiting for my eyes to adjust, I realized that I was looking at the snowcaps of the Olympic Mountains that form the backbone of the Olympic Peninsula. Some of those peaks rise to 8,000 feet, but compared to Rainier they seemed as nothing.

The next couple of miles wound in and out of pine groves. The summit of Rainier was now hidden by the crest of the ridge. The air took on the crisp feel of snow not far away. Sure enough, I began seeing snow patches in the pine groves; not enough to cover the ground, but enough to contribute to a noticeable drop in temperature.

Emerging from the shade once more, I glanced at my watch and saw that I had hit the six-mile mark. This was my turnaround point for today. I walked across the road and looked out over a south-facing bluff. Far below I could see a dirt logging road paralleling a narrow brook. Across the valley the South Cascades rippled away to the horizon. Mount Saint Helens was not quite in view. I had done it; six miles run, and 1500 feet in elevation climbed. With a smile, I turned and began the downhill leg of the run.

The sun had really begun to warm the air, and the view from high up on the ridgeline was magnificent. My leg muscles let go of all the tension from pushing uphill and fell into the easy, loping stride of downhill running. Movement felt effortless, like I was flying. Cresting the ridgeline, I descended to the Carbon River side. Before I knew it my car came into sight alongside the road, and just like that I was done.

I had made my pilgrimage to Mount Rainier, and the mountain had welcomed me.

CHAPTER 6

SPORTSMANSHIP

April 1977 | Northwood High School, Maryland

In my senior year of high school, I gave up the dream of playing varsity basketball. In my junior year tryouts I had made it all the way to the final cut, but this year focusing on studies in preparation for applying to college became the priority. I still played at lunchtime, and on an intramural team, and after school... I have always been, and always will be a gym rat.

With the basketball season long over, more of the varsity players started showing up in our pick-up games. This particular lunch time I was matched up against Doug Parker. Doug was a year younger than me, and 6'1" to my 6'5". He was also quicker and stronger than me, with a better vertical jump. On a typical day, Doug was a tough matchup for anyone. This day, however, Doug was having a terrible game. Jump shots clanged off the rim. On a fast break he dribbled off his foot and out of bounds.

Trash talking in basketball is a fine art that teenage boys have yet to master. I teased Doug, smug in my arrogance in that way that comes from the obliviousness of adolescence. Doug remained silent, but his temper was up. Towards the end of the game he missed an uncontested layup. I burst out laughing.

He turned on me. "You think that's funny, Stone? You want to put your money where that mouth of yours is? $25 says I can take you one on one any time."

The gym got very quiet, and the whole gathering crowd waited for me to respond. Sounding a lot more cocky than I suddenly felt, I said, "Sure. How about after school on Friday?"

With clenched jaw, Doug said, "You're on."

When Friday rolled around, word had spread. I entered the gym to find Doug waiting, and a small crowd of about a dozen. Half of them were his friends and teammates. The rest were just curious onlookers. I didn't have any friends in the audience; I hadn't even told my friends about the bet.

Our audience was quiet, and the thump of every basketball bounce echoed loudly through the gym. Whatever brief moment of anger I had provoked from Doug earlier in the week was gone. He was calm, polite even. Finally Doug paused, and asked, "Ready when you are?"

I nodded.

"First to 11, win by two, make it take it?" he inquired.

"Sure."

"Great. Let's shoot to see who starts with the ball."

Doug casually lofted a free throw; nothing but net. I stepped up and took my shot; the ball looped around the rim and rolled out. Doug took the ball and we started.

On defense I struggled to find the right approach. Doug was right handed, but I knew from playing with him in pick-up games that he was equally adept driving to his right or left. And he was quicker than me. So I started out playing him back. However, his best shot was really a little pull up jump shot from about twelve feet out. I was giving him too much room. So I started playing him tighter. Then, as expected, he used his quickness to drive by me.

On offense I struggled as well. I tried my staple turnaround jump shot from the right baseline, but he played very close on me, and my shot was off balance. I tried my crossover dribble, and he was overplaying me to the right so I got a good move on him, but missed the shot. Next time around he stripped the ball from me when I tried the crossover. I tried a quick pull up jump shot and he blocked it. I tried it again next time with a pump fake and he didn't go for the fake and blocked it again.

I came to the uncomfortable realization that I looked as inept on the court as Doug had looked on the day when my teasing had triggered the bet. I also recognized that my ineptitude had everything to do with Doug's skill on defense, whereas Doug's earlier poor performance was just Doug having a bad day. Yet Doug offered up no trash talking. He was quiet, businesslike.

Doug was still overplaying me to the right, so I worked us around to the left baseline. I started like I was going to drive across the middle of the lane, put a spin move on him and beat him around the left side, under the basket, for a reverse layup that he could not block with the basket in the way.

"Nice shot," he said, with genuine respect.

And so it went. Doug missed a few shots, but nothing I did defensively felt like it was working. I got an occasional good look at the basket, but the shots weren't falling, and every good look I created he adjusted to and took away from me. Finally down 9-1 I took him down to the right baseline for the mirror image of the move I scored on before, except that this time I did drive hard to the middle of the lane to put up a left-handed hook shot. Between my 4" height advantage and the geometry of the hook shot there was no way he could block it. The ball hit the center of the backboard with a satisfying thump and dropped through the basket. 9-2.

Doug shook his head, and said — again, with genuine appreciation — "Good move." He also scored the next two points with ease to win the game to applause from our small crowd.

I'm a man of my word, and I paid him his $25. He thanked me. We headed off the court, and the audience drifted away. I found myself a couple of steps ahead of Billy Kyle and muttered, "Well, that was embarrassing."

"Mark, are you kidding?"

I stopped, turned, and looked at him.

Billy smiled and said, "He told the rest of us he'd shut you out."

Monday morning at the start of the school day, Doug came up to me, a big grin on his face. "Check it out," he said, gesturing at his feet. "Brand. New. Shoes." Sure enough, he was sporting a nice pair of Puma basketball shoes. "Thanks man," he said, and then "See you around."

All of this took me a little time to process. I came from a middle class family, and I had a paper route to provide me with a little spending money. $25 was not a lot of money in my world. Doug came from an African American neighborhood that was politely described as working class. I was embarrassed to realize that I hadn't given much thought to what $25 meant in his world.

More importantly, Doug had taught me a lesson in humility. Humility in defeat is easy, yet runs the risk of sinking into discouragement. Humility in triumph is what a true sportsman demonstrates. Doug had been neither discouraged in defeat nor arrogant in triumph, and had shown me not just respect, but empathy. In fact, that empathy made him a stronger competitor. My adolescent brain, seething with hormones, hadn't entirely grasped this lesson, but a seed had been planted. My future self would one day embrace the idea that a community of athletes could be both deeply competitive and deeply empathetic.

And over the days and weeks ahead I found that I had a new friend. Indeed I enjoyed a new level of respect from the jocks at school. Finally, in one of life's nicer ironies, Doug and I would end up attending the same university, where our pick-up basketball games would continue.

CHAPTER 7

THE MOUNTAIN REBUKES ME

April 2013　|　Mount Rainier National Park

All week I kept thinking about my inaugural Rainier run. I had been so anxious about the elevation, the sustained uphill, the weather, and none of my fears had come to pass. I felt validated in the training plan I had devised, and eager to embrace the training season that lay before me. The weather deteriorated as the week wore on, but I hardly noticed. Yes, we had the typical spring drizzle of the Pacific Northwest. Yes, the temperature had dropped a few degrees. None of that dampened my enthusiasm. Early Saturday morning I practically bounded out of bed, grabbed my running gear, and headed out the door.

The plan for the day was to run the same route on Mount Rainier as the previous Saturday, only extending that from 12 miles to 15 miles. The same starting point as before offered me mist and drizzle, and temperatures in the high 40s. Not ideal conditions, but tolerable; the sort of weather we get a lot of in the Pacific Northwest, and the sort of weather you have to just accept if you're going to be a runner here.

I miscalculated, echoing my mistake in the Seattle Marathon. I assumed that as the morning progressed the temperature would rise and the weather would therefore improve. What I did not know was that the temperature would drop precipitously as I gained elevation, and that the ridgeline rising to my west was, for the moment, sheltering me from a strong winter storm blowing in off the Pacific.

Full of courage and naivete from the previous week's joyous run, I set off in shorts, no hat, no gloves, and a thin short sleeve t-shirt underneath a long sleeve shirt. As before, at about mile 4.5 I crossed over the ridge to the west slope, reaching about 2500 feet elevation.

Immediately I lost the wind shelter of the ridge itself; instead of a windless mist I was now running into winds gusting to 25 MPH. What I was running through could no longer be played down as drizzle, or even rain; it was a full on blizzard with huge, fat snowflakes.

Too late I realized that I was fighting a battle rather than taking in a run. When I hit the snow I almost turned back. My clothing was in no way suitable. I knew pressing on would be dangerous. But not hitting my distance for the day would really mess up my training schedule, or so I told myself. So I kept going. Stupid reason, I know, but there you have it.

I could actually feel my body shutting down to conserve energy. You know that feeling you get at the start of a cold run where your hands are just freezing and then the blood gets going and they warm up? I felt that. And then I felt the reverse of that. My hands, and then my feet got cold again. My brain simply said to my body, "Sorry, but these are not essential right now."

Then that feeling of cold crept up my arms, past my elbows. By the home stretch even my shoulders were starting to get numb. While I had food and water with me, I never took a break for either. It was one of those times when I felt like if I stopped for anything, I didn't know if I'd be able to start again. And motion was the only thing keeping me warm.

The first 20 minutes or so in the snow I kept saying to myself, "I should turn back. I'm going to turn back. It's not safe to keep going." But then the wind would drop, or I'd find shelter for a few moments as the road passed under trees, and I kept going.

Then I felt this strange shift in consciousness, like everything outside of my body was very far away, and I was just deep inside my head. Snow always muffles sound, and the moaning of the wind seemed to recede. The panorama of a storm rumbling through the Cascades was all around me, but I could only focus on the ten yards in front of me. I was in such a trance-like state that I almost overran my turnaround point and kept going without even realizing it.

Of course, whatever you can endure makes you stronger.

It wasn't the routine training run I had anticipated that day, but I learned something about myself getting through it. Most importantly I learned a deep respect for the mountain. Even as I write this now, that particular training run stands out as difficult and dangerous.

I vowed I would never underestimate the mountain again. Starting with the very next week I began driving up above the starting point of my run to scout out the conditions before driving back down to park at my starting point. Yet, as humbled as I was, the mountain would have more moments of humility in store for me in the future.

The run did have one humorous high point. Evans Creek Off Road Vehicle Park was the favorite playground of the local Jeep club. They met every Saturday morning, all year long, to play in whatever combination of rain, snow, or mud that nature had given them. They were there even on that stormy Saturday. As I came in sight of their parking area I dug in and cruised through with as much confidence as I could muster, calling out a cheerful "Good morning!" as I passed them by. One guy managed an "Um, hi?" as a reply. The rest of them just stared, their mouths hanging open. You'd think they had seen a unicorn.

CHAPTER 8

COUNTRY ROADS

1975 | Christ Congregational Church, Maryland

In every group of high school friends there is one star that shines brightest, around which the others seem to orbit. My group is the youth group for Christ Congregational Church of the United Church of Christ. Cyndy, Jane, Julie, Bill, and I came up together in the confirmation class of 1973. Our close friendship has drawn in kids our age — Lou, Ken, Lydia, her brother Alan, and her best friend Johnnie, Barry, Jane's brother Mark, Leslie, Richard, Kristen, and recent Chicago transplant Sergio.

Of all of us, it is Bill who burns brightest. He is handsome in a way that even the boys have to admire — deep blue eyes, straight jawed, jet black hair, and a frame that is athletic without being muscular, moving with the grace and ease of a cat. He is an academic standout, sings with perfect pitch, and plays guitar. Julie is his girlfriend, blonde, blue-eyed, also an academic standout and as much hippie chick as cheerleader.

The group of us has come of age in an odd time. The Sixties are over, but the social experiments of the epoch are still playing out in an unsure Seventies as society tries to figure out what it will keep and what it will discard from this turbulent time. Our church is a reflection of all of this. Our denomination emphasizes social action and stewardship, and has taken a strong stand on issues from civil rights to women's rights. Our congregation has almost been torn apart by the Vietnam War. The older members have a strong sense of loyalty and patriotism, born out of their experience of

World War II and the early days of the Cold War. The young adults are children of the Sixties, and adamantly anti-war.

Our youth group represents the next generation, with none of the baggage of these earlier generations, and little more than hope and innocence to guide us. And for our generation, youth has a power and freedom that will seem unattainable by the time the new millennium comes around. We are welcomed into the leadership of the church, serving on, or even chairing, the committees that do the church's work. We travel to the church's retreat house in West Virginia to participate in long weekend workshops on spirituality, individuality, and society. We take bare hands and energy otherwise spent tinkering on cars and bicycles to help renovate the aging retreat house; painting the front porch, building a new deck for the guest cottage, clearing undergrowth out of the back yard.

Through it all Bill is our ring leader, the Robin Hood of our merry band. He has a bold sincerity in his approach to life. Not many teens could sit at a campfire and deliver a John Denver song with complete conviction. Of course he's a rascal too, and we love him for it. He loves the angry protest songs of Bob Dylan, Stephen Stills, or Neil Young, and the Woodstock album is his favorite. So it is my favorite too. On our way to the retreat house one weekend we barrel through Winchester, Virginia with Bill leaning out of Barry's van singing the "Fish Song" from Woodstock at the top of his lungs, completely unconcerned that his talents might not be appreciated in this rural town south of the Mason Dixon line.

One afternoon, at the retreat house in West Virginia, Bill invites me — just me — on a long hike with him, and I feel so privileged to be chosen. We saunter out the retreat house door, follow the road down to the river, and after wading across, clamber up Baker Mountain on the far side. The trail we're following is an old road long abandoned, now nothing more than a grassy pathway through the trees. The sounds of cars and the other clatter of human activity have long since faded into the distance as we stroll through the heavy quiet of a summer afternoon. We talk of Tolkien, and "The Lord of the Rings", which each of us has only recently read for the first time.

Bill pauses, and looks through the trees out over the valley below. "It could be Rivendell", he says.

In that moment I understand Tolkien's concept of magic for the first time. To Tolkien magic is not something alien and otherworldly. It's the opposite. It is the very feel of this world distilled to an intensity we are seldom aware of. Yet Bill and I, alone in the West Virginia mountains, can feel it. Right there, before our eyes, at our fingertips, magic is all around us.

To hike for miles, to climb the hills, to descend into nature far removed from human touch, and to discover the purity of the primordial world that awaits... On this day Bill and I have planted a seed that will germinate within me for many years to come.

CHAPTER 9

PUSHING BOUNDARIES

May 2013　|　Mount Rainier National Park

The calendar moved from winter to spring, and reached towards summer. Yet with each run on Mount Rainier I found winter waiting somewhere on the upper slopes.

Early on Saturday mornings I would park my car in the quiet, gray light surrounded by mist, or the steady drizzle of rain. Buds hesitantly probed forth from branches, and the bright green of new leaves made an ever denser canopy above me. In the muffled morning air the only sound would be the crunch of gravel beneath my shoes as I began with a slow jog up the slope. Soon I would pass from leafy oaks to the solemn shadow of the tall pines, their dark green needles unmoved by the change of seasons.

Higher up the sounds would change. The occasional cry of a hawk would pierce the air, solitary and mournful. When I scanned the skies I would sometimes glimpse a flash of the white of a bald eagle's head. I would hear the quiet trickle of water that signaled the beginning of snow melt. As I moved higher still, to where rocky promontories began to jut through the pines, I would hear the bubbling rush of little waterfalls tumbling down the rocks.

Then I would catch the smell, a crisp freshness in the air, that signaled I was approaching snow. First I would see just a patch here or there, along with ice covering the road side puddles. Finally I would round a bend in the road — each week a different bend, a little higher — only to find snow all the way across the road. I knew that somewhere beyond the snow line the road ended at Mowich Lake. Always I turned around miles before that destination, and descended once again to my car in the long, loping strides that are the joy of downhill running.

On the rare sunny days, I could see the snowcap of Mount Rainier's summit dodging in and out of view, depending on the intervening ridgeline and trees. Some days patches of clouds would cling to the mountain tops, obscuring my view of the summit. Then the wind would assert itself, pulling back the cloudy curtain for a dazzling glimpse of Rainier's magnificence that would always bring me up short to simply stare in awe. Even on the days when cloud and rain completely obscured the summit, I felt the presence of the mountain, looming just beyond sight.

When I began my Mount Rainier runs, I thought of the mountain as a solitary place. That spring, however, I came to realize that Rainier has its own community of pilgrims who regularly sojourn on its slopes, each to appreciate the mountain in their own way.

The folks I saw most often were the Jeep club. Then there were the hikers. In these months they adapted as cross country skiers, snow shoers, and the occasional snow boarder.

The height of spring was also mating season for elk. Through the pines I could hear the woofing snort of a female, or the distant bugling of a bull. One morning, as I approached a father and his teenage son pulled off on the side of the road, the man beckoned me over. He pointed down the slope, and handed me a pair of binoculars. Sure enough, a magnificent buck stood in the clearing, his rack of pronged antlers on full display. Rummaging in his backpack, the man pulled out a camera with zoom lens. With a glance at his son, he smiled and said, "These days this is all I shoot with."

Once in a while the fortress of snow would get the better of me, and I'd find myself laying siege to it. On this particular morning late in May, I'd been away from the mountain for a few weeks and I felt sure the way to Mowich Lake would at last be passable. I reached the parking area and check point, where a metal gate closed off the road to vehicles. For half of the year, from November until June, the gate is closed because the road beyond is impassable until the snow level has receded. For most of this closure time the gate itself is irrelevant, because the snow level extends far lower than the gate itself.

So far, I had seen only patches of snow. A mile further on, the snow fully covered the road, but I could still find bare patches under the shadow of the great pines to make progress. Within a half mile those bare patches had vanished, and the snow deepened. Each attempted stride sunk me in up to my ankles, and then up to my shins. Finally I came out of my runner's daze, pulled up, and looked around. The lake was at least two miles further, and I doubted I could make another hundred yards. Like Tolkien's Fellowship on Caradhras, the mountain had denied me and turned me back.

Mowich Lake sits at 5000 feet elevation. I had reached the impassable snow line at roughly 3500 feet, about the same elevation as the starting line for the Winthrop Marathon, now less than a month away. Was this what I had signed up for?

Rainier to
Ruston Relay
Fairfax

CHAPTER 10

SASQUATCH

June 2012 | Mount Rainier National Park

The Pacific Northwest boasts several popular relay races. Ski to Sea near the Canadian border has relay teams engaged in a multi-sport competition that includes skiing, cycling, running, and kayaking as teams make their way from the North Cascades to the ocean. The most popular is the 200 mile Hood to Coast, in which relay teams run from the slopes of Mount Hood outside of Portland all the way to the Oregon Coast.

My favorite, though, is the Rainier to Ruston, which passes through my neighborhood and covers trails on which I have spent many miles. Close to 2000 runners participate each year, most organized into teams of six. A runner completes a stage, hands off to the next runner, and the team rotates in this manner through all twelve stages. The start is at the Carbon River entrance to Mount Rainier; the finish is in the Tacoma waterfront park along Ruston Way.

On this sunny June day my first experience of this race would be as a volunteer. The logistical challenge with the relay is that you cannot fit all 2000 runners and their vehicles at a checkpoint at the same time. To make things manageable, runners start in waves. I was assigned to Checkpoint 1, the handoff between the first and second stages of the race.

I left the house early that morning, eager to see something of the starting area before settling into my assigned volunteer post. When I reached the Carbon River entrance to Mountain Rainier National Park, the grassy field that served as a temporary parking lot was already busy. Relay teams were assembling, and the air filled with the chatter and laughter of runners eager to start. And of course everyone wanted their picture taken with the race's unofficial mascot, the costumed volunteer dressed as Sasquatch. Having had my taste of race atmosphere, I headed back down the mountain to my post.

Upon my arrival I was greeted by Jim, a long time volunteer of Foothills Trail Coalition. We had about an hour until the first runners would arrive, and already the checkpoint was buzzing with activity. Volunteers had snacks and water ready at a table. Other volunteers stood ready to monitor the handoff zone, where runners would pass the baton. Other volunteers stood on the far side of the bridge over the Carbon River to direct runners off of the road and onto the narrow, single track dirt trail that makes up most of Stage 2.

Jim introduced me to a woman named Pat, and explained that the two of us would be supervising the parking area. Pat, it seemed, was a long time volunteer. As we chatted, it came to light that she was in fact the mayor of Buckley, my home town.

In fact, Buckley was sponsoring a team of runners, as they apparently did every year. Pat explained that this was part of a friendly competition between the mayors of the towns through which the race passed: Buckley, Orting, Puyallup, and Fife. The stakes? A case of Rainier Beer. Pat had worked hard to bring in some "ringers" this time, some of the faster local trail runners. Like the other mayors, she was raising money for charity through her team, in her case support for the local Buckley youth center.

About this time the first vehicles showed up. Rainier to Ruston is as much a festival on wheels as it is a race. Runners pick humorous names for their teams, like "Honeybuckets", "Long Distance Relay-tionship", or "Legs Miserables". Often they get t-shirts printed up for the team, and vehicles are festooned with signs and banners. Following Pat's lead, I could see that there was an art to organizing parking. Drivers wanted to park by the front of the grassy field we had to work with, so they could get in and out quickly, but we couldn't let too many cars pile up in the front without making the rest of the field inaccessible. Pat had a politician's knack for friendly engagement but firm guidance. She projected authority without ruffling feathers.

Once parked, teams piled out of their cars and hurried to the exchange point. The first runners came into view, loping down the long, curving road as it descended towards the bridge. Teammates cheered, some rang cowbells, and with a hasty exchange the next runner would be off.

Pat and I found that we didn't quite have enough time between waves. The last cars still trickled out of the parking area from the first wave as cars for second wave runners started to arrive. A couple of times we had to instruct drivers to back up and make room for someone else to pass. Through it all Pat never lost her composure or her smile.

By the time the final wave passed through, I felt like I had mastered the system. The last car pulled away, and suddenly it felt very quiet. It was about 10:00 in the morning, and the relay would continue until sunset as teams worked their way across the 50 miles of trail. Our part was done. Jim came up and thanked me for volunteering.

He said, "If you have time this evening, we have a little get together for the volunteers at the beer garden at the finish area. You should stop by."

And so I did. 6:00 that evening saw the last runners reaching the finish line. Sasquatch, of course, was there to greet them. Many of these were ultra runners, who had run the entire 50 miles solo. I stepped into the beer garden, and was handed a mug. I chatted a bit with other volunteers from other exchange points, everyone sharing stories of their favorite team name or costume they saw that day. Then I saw Pat. All she had in her hand was a glass of water.

She waved as I approached, and I inquired, "No beer?"

Her smile spread into a big grin and she said, "Oh, I've got a whole case coming my way. First place, baby!"

CHAPTER 11

YOU CAN'T ALWAYS GET WHAT YOU WANT

1974　｜　Washington D.C.

Over the last year I spent eight months growing eleven inches, from 5'3" to 6'2". The last few months have involved a week at the University of Maryland basketball camp, hours of additional practice and pick-up games, and a lot of time just trying to figure out this new sized body my brain finds itself within. Under the steady hand of a good coach at the local Boys' Club, I am starting to find my way.

Today's game is shaping up to be a challenge. With my mom helping out with the carpooling, we've brought six boys, from a roster of ten, in from suburban Maryland to play a road game in a very working class inner city neighborhood.

Just before tip-off Coach Dave pulls me aside for a quick word. "You aren't going to get a lot of rest this game. These other kids play with gusto, but I can't count on them to have a lot of stamina."

I nod, not really sure what to say.

He looks me in the eye. "Play steady. I'm counting on you."

The first half goes like many of our games. There's Tommy, who's about two inches shorter than me but very athletic. If he gets the ball down low he can score on a fair number of his acrobatic moves, and he's a menace on the offensive boards. Then there's Duane, our shooting guard, who never saw a jump shot he didn't like. He has a nice touch, but he has no discipline staying inside the offense to work for open shots.

For my part I dutifully float down court under the basket, and then double back up to the high post looking for any entry pass we can turn into a pick and roll or a give and go. By and large my efforts to run the plays go ignored. At the end of the half I have a meager two assists, no shots taken, we trail by four, and the rest of the guys are looking winded.

Coach Dave is not happy. "Come on! We practice these plays every day. Now run the offense. Mark is the only one out there following the plays."

This outburst is met with mostly downcast eyes, except for Duane who gives an exaggerated eye roll. Coach turns on him, and shouts, "You follow the plays or I'll bench you. Any one of you." Turning to me with the remnants of his temper he says, "Demand the ball out there. Show some authority."

The second half starts with better discipline. I touch the ball on each possession as we go on a quick 8-0 run. But we're all tired, and the fatigue is starting to show. I've been in the whole game and Coach shows no sign of taking me out. The minutes flow by and the game seesaws back and forth. Duane resorts to more gunslinging, and Tommy's fatigue is costing him on the boards.

I try my best to rally the team. "Give me the ball!" I yell as I step up to the top of the key. Startled, Duane obliges, and, staring in his direction, I drop a no look pass to Jimmy, shortest guy on the team who hardly ever gets the ball. For a moment he bobbles it, but there's no one between him and the basket and he nails a short jumper.

Next time down we run the setup again. "Come on!" I yell, and again Duane dishes off to me. This time the other team is hesitating, not sure who I'll go to. Duane flashes by his man and I hit him in full stride with a bounce pass that he converts into an easy layup.

With about two minutes to go we find ourselves up by two. I'm getting tighter coverage in the high post now, and so the guys are working the ball around the perimeter looking for an opening. Suddenly one of the defenders jumps on a telegraphed pass, nabs the ball, and takes off down court. I sprint after him. There's no one between him and the basket.

Our chase feels like one of those slow motion moments. No one on the court but the two of us moves. I'm closing the gap between us, but he's closing on the basket, the sound of his dribble echoing through the gym like a heartbeat. Thump. Thump. Thump. I'm close now, as he's about to stretch for a layup. "Time it, time it," I think to myself. He leaps, and I leap. Just as the ball leaves his fingertips my hand slaps it from behind. Bam! The ball careens off the backboard and bounces back towards half court.

At the far end of the court my teammates erupt in cheers, while the opposing team stands there stunned. Jimmy has the presence of mind to scoop up the ball. We're up by two, and the clock is winding down through the last minute.

Alas, our moment is brief. Jimmy is fouled, and makes one of two shots. The opposition puts up a quick two points on a mid range jumper. As we bring the ball down Duane throws it away trying to hit Tommy down in the low post. With less than ten seconds to go the opposition misses another jumper, but Tommy, who is beyond fatigued now, is flat footed on the rebound and their power forward tips it in. We're down by one. Duane dribbles the ball off his foot and out of bounds as time runs out, trying to force a drive where there's no opening.

Just like that we've lost. Coach played me the entire game, and I am tired, so tired. What do I have to show for his trust? Maybe a dozen rebounds, half a dozen assists, 0 for 2 from the field, no points scored. And we've been defeated. Eyes downcast, I walk towards the sidelines.

A voice stops me. It's the referee, jogging over to me.

"Son," he says, "you played a heck of a game. That's as fine a game as I've seen played in a long time."

I nod, not really understanding, and mumble thanks.

He smiles, and as he turns away, says, "Your coach obviously has a lot of faith in you. You earned it today."

Out of defeat, triumph can be born. The choice is ours.

CHAPTER 12

THE TALE OF BOB HOEKMAN

June 2013 | Winthrop, Washington

The Winthrop Marathon did not turn out as I had hoped. Yet on the morning after, somehow that didn't seem important.

One of the things I absolutely love about the running community is those spontaneous moments of camaraderie we strike up with total strangers on race day. So my account of the Winthrop Marathon is really the tale of Bob Hoekman.

The starting line is reached via a one hour bus ride from Winthrop. The start is deep in the Okanogan National Forest, on a steel bridge crossing the Chewuch River with an elevation of about 3000 feet. The road parallels the river back down the mountainside, breaking out of the woods around Mile 16 and transitioning to the high, open pasture common in this area. At this point the elevation is about 1500 feet, and the course is rolling hills and grassland the rest of the way. You reach the town of Winthrop at Mile 23, then do a 1.5 mile out and back on the south side of town, make a sharp U turn upon returning to town, and finish on the main street. Start time temperature was about 50 degrees, but once out in the open the temperature ranged from mid 70s to 80 under a cloudless sky.

My plan had been to run a fast start over the first ten miles to take advantage of the steepest downhills, and then to ease off and take a much more relaxed pace with lots of breaks and walking as needed over the last 16 miles. I certainly hadn't forgotten that I was completely out of energy at the end of the Seattle Marathon and craving Gatorade as the only thing that would get me through to the finish. So I took 20 oz of Gatorade in my fuel belt to provide a late race supplement in addition to what the aid stations provided along the way.

I ran a great race for 22 miles. At mile 10 I was under 9 minutes per mile, and I was disciplined enough to take that down to about 10 minutes per mile over the next section; a little faster on the downhills, a little slower on the uphills. At Mile 22 my time was 3 hours and 50 minutes, well ahead of my Seattle Marathon pace and seemingly on track for my desired finishing time of under 4 hours 30 minutes.

But I did not account for the relentless and cumulative effect of the heat, dry air, and sun. I craved water more and more. Mile 22 arrived at the end of a gradual but lengthy 2 mile uphill grade, and as I staggered through to Mile 23, I realized I was spent. I was feeling a bit of a headache, a bit nauseous, with a growing tingling sensation around my scalp. The gatorade in my fuel belt did not appeal to me at all, and all I wanted was to get to the next aid station and water. Heat stroke was not something I was willing to risk, so I slowed to a walk, and then to an even slower walk. It took me 25 minutes to cover Mile≈24, and another 25 minutes to cover Mile≈25. Finally my body had recovered enough to resume a slow jog, and I covered the last 1.2 miles in 14 minutes.

There's nothing quite like the feeling of turning the corner for the finish line and seeing your family waiting there for you. People were clapping and cheering, but the only thing I heard was my son Nathan yelling, "Mom! Mom! It's Dad!" A week early, but it was the best Father's Day present ever. Finishing time: 4 hours 54 minutes.

But enough about me. At Mile 2 this guy pulled up next to me, and as we seemed to be at about the same pace we settled in running side by side. After a hundred yards or so of this, he said, "Good morning! I'm Bob Hoekman, and I'm from Houston, Texas."

Glancing at Bob, he was clearly older than me, but I wouldn't have said by much. My guess would have been late 50s or early 60s. And he was hard to miss.

He stood about 6' 3" and was wearing a fluorescent yellow running shirt.

I introduced myself and we ran quietly together.

After a minute or so, Bob commented, "Not sure how I'm going to do today. This is my fourth marathon this year, and my legs are a little tired."

"Well this is my second marathon ever," I replied. "I started running again when I was 49."

"How old are you now?"

"I'm 53."

"Well good for you," Bob said enthusiastically. "I started running again when I was 46."

I had to ask, "How old are you now?"

Bob grinned, and said, "I'm 71."

There was silence for a bit while I digested that information. Then I said humbly, "I hope I'm still running marathons when I'm 71."

Bob let out a big laugh, and said, "I hope I'm still running marathons when I'm 91!"

And so we ran and chatted from Mile 2 to about Mile 7. Bob hales from Texas, but had a home in the Winthrop area, and this was his third time running the Winthrop Marathon. He'd also run the entire course as a training run. His last race was in Kalamazoo, Michigan, where he and his wife were visiting his mother-in-law. I didn't ask how old she was.

Around Mile 7 our paces began to get out of sync, and we separated a bit. But Bob was always easy to spot with that bright yellow shirt, and he was never out of sight either in front of or behind me. At Mile 13 we passed the half marathon start, and, slow and steady, Bob and I began passing the tail of the half marathon pack. Around Mile 17 it was me catching up to him, and I asked "How are you doing?"

"Not so well," he acknowledged. "I've been battling a viral infection, and actually thought about skipping this race. But I woke up without a fever this morning, so I figured I'd give it a shot."

I pulled in for a water break and some food at Mile 18, and Bob soldiered on. At Mile 20 I spotted his yellow shirt up ahead. He was walking with a young, attractive, and very fit brunette. As I squinted at the glaring sun overhead it seemed to me like a good time to take a walking break too, so I slowed down next to them.

Bob grinned, and said, "I've had a bit of an irregular heart beat, so I'm taking it easy. This is Holly. She's a nurse, and she's looking after me."

Holly and I introduced ourselves. She was mainly a trail runner, a CrossFit / Tough Mudder / Warrior Dash type, never having run anything over 10 miles. She had signed up for the half marathon on a whim.

Some ten minutes later Holly and I had resumed running, and pulled a bit ahead of Bob. I asked, "Is he going to be okay?"

She rolled her eyes, and gave me a look of complete disgust. "He's a doctor," she said. "They make the worst patients! But don't worry, I'll keep an eye on him."

I pushed on, leaving Holly and Bob behind. I stopped looking around, getting that tunnel vision that comes with end of race focus and fatigue. But sure enough, at Mile 25, as I was in my own struggle to keep putting one foot in front of the other, Bob jogged by me, huffing and puffing. He had tunnel vision too; I don't think he even saw me. But then he hit the turnaround point on the out and back, and we passed each other again, this time in opposite directions. He looked up, saw me struggling, and gave me that big Texan smile and a thumbs up. That certainly made my day, and it was just the boost I needed.

Bob finished about three minutes ahead of me, with a time of 4 hours, 51 minutes, and 13 seconds; a true testament to running for a lifetime.

CHAPTER 13

RUNNER BORN

1973 | Silver Spring, Maryland

"Come on, you long-legged dork! Run! Run your ass off!" The kids from the first heat are screaming and yelling at me from the sidelines. The words are all too familiar, but the tone is different: exhorting instead of deriding, respect instead of mockery. As I cross the finish line the P.E. teacher calls out "72 seconds."

A glance over my shoulder shows no one within a hundred yards of me. I'm mad. I'm absolutely furious. Because I know I can do so much better. And for the first time, the kids on the sidelines know it too.

We are doing track and field in P.E., my first formal experience with it. We've just completed the 440 yard dash. Our teacher separated us into two groups which basically amounted to the jocks and the nerds. The jock group had run first, with times ranging from 58 to 80 seconds. I wanted to be in that group, because I knew I could run with them. Without someone to push me, I know my own time is substandard.

It proves to be a pivotal moment, though. Two weeks later we do cross country running, a two-mile course through Sligo Creek Parkway, and I finish in the top 3. In the eyes of my peers I have begun to change. It will be a gradual change, but it will continue all through junior high and high school. Less and less I am labeled a hopeless nerd, and more and more seen as a brainy jock.

I love basketball and tennis, and have begun to excel at basketball. But I love running the most, and running cross country more than anything else. In the years ahead my interests will wander. At age 13, activities like backpacking and rock climbing, that will become major pursuits, are still in my future. Yet, no matter how far my interests stray, as the years slip by, I always return to running. This mere two-mile run is a small beginning, but a profound one.

From across a gulf of 40 years my future self will look back on this moment and thank the scrappy youngster that I am for embracing the grit and challenge of endurance running.

olumbia

CHAPTER 14

HEAR MY TRAIN A COMIN'

July 2013 | Beaverton, Oregon

"Over the years, I've given myself a thousand reasons to keep running, but it always comes back to where it started. It comes down to self-satisfaction and a sense of achievement." — Steve Prefontaine

About two weeks after the Winthrop Marathon, my professional and running life took a sudden turn. I secured a one year contract position — a contract-to-hire opportunity — with Nike's Digital Sports Division at the company headquarters in Beaverton, Oregon.

The job was hard on my family. With a permanent position not yet secured, we couldn't commit to relocating. So on Sunday evenings I would take the train from Tacoma down to Portland, spend the week at a tiny apartment I had rented in Beaverton, and then take the train back on Friday afternoon.

Though I didn't know it at the time, this job would end a period of ten years in which I'd had several extended periods of layoffs and unemployment. In February of the following year I would leave Nike to return to the Seattle area for a permanent position with Disney Corporate Technology Services Group. My family's financial status was finally secure.

Nike also introduced me to the world of Portland area running. These days Nike is such a pervasive presence in all sports that it's easy to forget that the company was created by and for runners. Nike was founded in 1964 by

Phil Knight, a varsity track runner of modest ability at the University of Oregon. Starting with legendary coach Bill Bowerman, the University of Oregon has been the premier track and field school in the NCAA. Bowerman's experimentations with running shoe design led him to be a collaborator and co-founder of Nike with Phil Knight.

Nike's first sponsored athlete was a Coos Bay native, the fiercely competitive and highly charismatic Steve Prefontaine. During his career he held American records at every distance from 2,000 to 10,000 meters. He was the first runner to attain true celebrity status, amplified by his tragic death in a car crash at age 24. Prefontaine did as much as any single individual to put Portland, Oregon on the map as a destination for serious runners.

Nike's headquarters is surrounded by an earthen wall, known as "The Berm", designed to keep prying eyes from the general public and paparazzi away from the star athletes that visit and workout there. Atop the Berm is a 1.6 mile track. During the time I worked there, lunchtime runs on the Berm were crowded, and could mean a chance encounter with anyone from a co-worker to Mo Farah. The campus also featured an Olympic standard quarter mile track, tucked away in a grove of trees — again, putting the privacy of athletes first. The whole campus is a temple to athleticism, with banners and statues featuring sponsored athletes. Yet only Steve Prefontaine has a dedicated shrine — Prefontaine Hall.

The atmosphere at Nike was energizing, even for an ordinary runner. Most days included at least a short run at lunchtime. Even when I told my manager, "I'm going out for a run; I'll be back in a couple of hours" he'd just smile and nod, as if to say, "Of course you are." Our building, in a drab office park outside the main campus, had a full weight room, and a full-sized indoor basketball court.

Yet it was really beyond the Nike campus that I found my greatest inspiration as a runner.

Situated at the confluence of the Willamette and Columbia Rivers, Portland is a city of hills. The west side of Portland runs up the slopes of the Tualatin Mountains, and straddling the Tualatin ridgeline is one of America's great urban parks — Forest Park. Eight miles in length, 5100 acres overall, Forest Park offers up rugged, unspoiled pine forest criss-crossed by mostly single track dirt trails. It is a runners' paradise. The most popular trail, the Leif Erikson Trail, is wide, relatively flat, and measured by prominent granite markers that call out the miles in quarter mile increments. At ten miles in length, for a 20 mile out and back, you could do the entirety of training for a marathon on the Leif Erikson.

To me the jewel of Forest Park will always be the Wildwood Trail. 31 miles of narrow single track, the Wildwood swoops from the lowest stream beds to the highest ridges, with endless switchbacks in and out of the furrowed slopes of the Tualatin Mountains. Even a moderate long run on the Wildwood could involve a couple thousand feet of elevation gain. My early ventures onto the lower slopes of Mount Rainier that spring had involved grades up to 5% and elevation gain in the 1000 to 1500 foot range. Wildwood was a challenge of a whole different level.

And it was a challenge to which I responded. By October of that year I was in the best running shape of my life.

October 2013
Portland, Oregon

One of my 2013 goals was to set a new PR for the half marathon. After a busy race season in the first half of the year (two 10Ks, a half marathon, and a full marathon), my entire training focus from June was to run a great half marathon in the fall. I would be running in a new city — Portland — and "Run Like Hell" looked like a fun event covering some classic Portland running routes (Riverfront, Terwilliger Hill).

The route starts in downtown Portland at Pioneer Courthouse Square, winds through a flat stretch of city streets, and then along the greenway adjacent to the Willamette River. At about Mile 3 the route begins a gradual climb as the course approaches Terwiliger Hill, and then from Mile 5 to Mile 7 there's a fairly steep climb with about 500 feet of elevation gain to the hilltop. The course follows a different route down the hill with a mostly straight, gradual descent from Mile 7 to about Mile 10.5. Then it's back along the river, back through downtown to finish at Pioneer Courthouse Square.

Like many tall runners (I'm 6'5"), I'm not a great hill runner. Sure, I love to stretch out my stride and pick up the pace on the downhills, but challenging uphills have been my bane. As I first noticed at the Seattle Marathon, I've struggled with recurrent tightness in my left hamstring; it flares up most frequently under high intensity running (like running uphill).

My race plan was to start out somewhat below my target pace, beginning at something like 9:15 a mile, to ease off as much as my left hamstring needed me to on the uphill part, and then to open up the throttle on the long downhill to something more like 8:20 a mile, hoping to sustain that increased pace through the downtown flats back to the finish line. The challenge would be to climb Terwilliger Hill without losing too much pace but also without expending too much energy.

My training plan was routine at this point: four days a week of running that include a long slow run and short slow run on consecutive days, a tempo run day trying to keep the pace under 8:45 per mile, and an intervals day on the treadmill that is mix of 1/4 mile intervals and 1/8 mile hill intervals. My long run tops out at 15 miles when training for a half marathon, my tempo run tops out at eight miles, and my weekly mileage tops out at about 36 miles per week.

During training, I felt like I was still building off a strong base from my build-up to the Winthrop Marathon in the first half of the year. After Winthrop, and after shifting to the Portland area, I continued extensive hill work by going regularly out to Forest Park and running on the Wildwood Trail (the low and high points on Wildwood differ by about 700 feet in elevation).

While the distance in a half marathon doesn't phase me any more, I always worry about my ability to summon up and sustain a decent pace.

In my peak intensity week of training I turned in an eight-mile run in just over an hour, so I was feeling pretty confident heading into my taper period.

Race morning arrived, thankfully without rain or wind. It was cold (low 40s) and foggy at the start, and would remain that way throughout. Staying warm before the start was a little challenging (thank you, Starbucks), but I wasn't worried about the cold once we got moving. I made several significant changes in my race plan compared to previous half marathons.

- First, I made a calculated choice not to stop at any of the water stations. Two hours in cold weather is not enough time to become dehydrated if you've hydrated properly ahead of time, even when you're pushing yourself.

- Second, and related, I was determined to avoid bathroom breaks. It's just time wasted, and shouldn't be necessary in a two-hour event.

- Third, I changed up my race fuel strategy. I brought along a handful of chocolate-covered espresso beans to be consumed right before the start, figuring the carbs and the caffeine would be a good boost. And I pocketed a couple of salt water taffies as my only in-race fuel, to be consumed right as I approached the top of Terwilliger Hill. Yes, I'd have to slow down to a walk to eat, but it was an ideal place in the race to slow down and catch my breath.

- Finally, I ran with a GPS watch (Nike+ SportWatch) for the first time ever. My race plan called for paying careful attention to pace through each stage of the race.

So, that was the plan.

We had about 800 runners at the start, and I positioned myself about two-thirds of the way back in the corral. Given my expected time I should probably have been farther forward, but I like the feeling of passing people. I felt good through the first couple of miles, keeping some spring in my step but not going out too fast. As we left the riverfront and angled uphill, I noted that my pace to that point was 9:25 / mile, slower than desired because of time spent clearing the crowd coming out of the corral. Even though we were starting up hill at this point, I took a chance and picked up my pace. So far my hamstring seemed to be responding well. I'd really changed my running form a lot in the last year, getting away from the long, loping stride I'd used for so many years and focusing a faster turnover with short, quick strides. By the end of Mile 5 I was back on pace, averaging 9:10 / mile to that point.

The next two miles would be the tough part. I slowed considerably, but tried not to slow my cadence. Basically my strides just got shorter and shorter. Along this stretch I was barely putting one foot ahead of the other, and really had to run looking at my feet to make sure I didn't step on my own foot. The grade along this stretch was about 4%, and I really didn't find it too bad. I kept thinking back to my spring runs on Mount Rainier, where a 5% to 6% grade would just go on for miles. Indeed I found that I was passing a lot of people on Terwilliger Hill, and that my breathing was pretty even compared to the huffing and puffing I heard all around me. The hill tops out on a sweeping curve that brings you around to the long, straight downhill and as I rounded onto that curve I pulled up at last, slowing to a walk to take my taffy break. At this point my overall pace had dropped to 9:25 / mile. Pretty much right where I wanted to be, but I was going to need sub-8:30 miles the rest of the way to hit a PR. Did I have enough left in the tank to keep up that kind of pace?

I picked up the pace aggressively in the next mile (8:23), and then flew down the next two miles of the downhill section (8:02 and 7:55). I hit the flats, and focused on keeping up the pace (8:11). Yes, I was working hard, and yes I could feel the strain, but I felt good. At this point I had less than two miles to go, and I knew there was no way I was going to let up this close to the finish.

And then...

The train.

Yes, there is indeed a freight train line that runs through downtown Portland, and the race organizers warn you up front on the website that train delays are a possibility. They have timing mats set up right before and right after the tracks, and do their best to count only your moving time and not time spent waiting for a train. And indeed most races it isn't even an issue. But this time it was an issue. A big issue. Because the train we were all bunching up in front of wasn't even moving.

It turns out one of the freight car sensors had sent a "wheel off the track" alert (in error this time), which mandates an immediate halt. The crew then had to walk the length of the train (two miles, roughly) and check every wheel. This process took 30 minutes. Thirty minutes during which I was standing still, in 40-something degree weather, soaked in my own sweat, developing a chill as my muscles tightened up further and further. Many runners gave up and just wandered off through side streets back towards downtown. But not me. I was determined to get an official time out of this one way or another. I had trained four months for this event, and I was not giving up. Finally the train began to move. We then waited another ten minutes for the train to clear the crossing. We had been waiting so long that my GPS watch, which I had paused, gave up. Surely I couldn't still be running, it must have figured.

At last the train was clear, and we all lurched forward. I don't know how fast I ran those last 1.75 miles, but I do know that I was angry, furious even, and I just channeled all that fury into my effort. My legs were stiff and cramping, I had to shake off a shiver from the chill in my shoulders, but I didn't care. "Just run. You can rest later. You have six months at least until your next race. Just run." That was what I kept saying to myself over and over through the home stretch. I turned the last corner with about a 200 yard straightaway between me and the finish line and felt like I was completely spent. Somehow I managed to dig deeper into that anger and the next thing I knew I found myself sprinting, all the way to the finish line and across.

Officially my time was 1 hour 54 minutes and 57 seconds. That's 1 minute and 23 seconds better than my previous PR. Part of me feels like there's an asterisk next to that time, on account of the train. But most of me feels like this:

It doesn't matter what my time was. I know in my heart that I ran my best half marathon ever, and I don't need a clock time to validate that. The external confirmation is nice, but not necessary. I know how I felt, I know how I ran, and I know what I accomplished.

If anything, I'm grateful to be reminded of the uniqueness of each race. No two courses are the same, and given the variables of weather and other runners present on that particular day, even the same race is not really the same from one year to the next. Whatever triumph we feel, whatever struggle we endure, we must understand it as both unique to the moment of that particular race, and yet essential to the whole of who we are as runners. And so I leave you with a quote from someone far more eloquent than I'll ever be, in both words and deed, when it comes to running. Each day when I started work at Nike, I would see a photo of this man when I entered the front door of the building. And next to the photo it said:

"A race is a work of art that people can look at and be affected in as many ways they're capable of understanding." — Steve Prefontaine

DOWN IN THE VALLEY

December 2005 | Modesto, California

Bounded on one side by the coastal foothills, and on the other side by the Sierra Nevadas, California's Central Valley is like a big bowl hundreds of miles long. In the winter months especially it is often subject to thermal inversion, creating a thick blanket of ground level fog. As I descended from Sonora to the valley floor, I encountered the fog. I was exhausted. And anxious. And I could barely see. At a certain point I effectively lost sight of the road and could only follow the tail lights of the car in front of me. As I trailed the ambulance to the hospital on that bleak December night, I struggled through darkness like I'd never felt before.

Five years earlier, I had decided to do the financially prudent thing and buy a house. Though I was a rising professional in Silicon Valley, I was also a recently divorced father dutifully paying child support. I knew I could not afford a house in the Bay Area. So I reframed the problem. A house is mainly a place to store our possessions, most of which we don't need on a daily basis. Thus a Bay Area house was not only an expensive storage facility, but an unnecessary one for my few possessions. Somewhere nearby would be good enough. Somewhere nearby would also give me a weekend destination away from the urban sprawl that surrounded me.

How nearby was near enough? I decided a three hour drive was reasonable, something I'd be willing to undertake on a Friday evening after work, and something I could do on a Sunday that wouldn't wear me out. Looking at a map, I drew a circle with a three hour radius centering on Silicon Valley, and considered locations that were both appealing and within my budget. Marin, Sonoma, or Napa? Too expensive. Santa Cruz or Monterey? Still too expensive. The Central Valley from Sacramento to Fresno? Unappealing. That left two possibilities: Clear Lake, just over the hills from Napa and Sonoma, or Sonora, a little Gold Rush era town in the foothills between the Central Valley and the Sierra Nevadas. For an outdoors enthusiast like me, being situated at the gateway to the Sierras had tremendous appeal. So, in the spring of 2000 I began what would be a months long process of occasional trips up to Sonora to look at real estate.

During these trips I stayed in a hotel right downtown. The ground floor had a restaurant and a karaoke bar. While I'm no singer, the bar offered a comfortable place to hang out and relax, and begin to get to know the locals. Laurie, who was about my age, managed the bar and tended bar sometimes. Christina, who was a good bit younger, tended bar regularly, while her younger sister Barbie handled karaoke. Barbie and I even went out a few times, but settled on friendship over romance.

Work took me out of California and away for a good bit of the fall. I returned to find that my realtor had found a place that I was absolutely in love with. Five and a half acres of land at 4000 feet elevation, with a panoramic view out over the Central Valley and adjacent to the wilderness of Stanislaus National Forest. The property had an aging double-wide trailer, but there was lots of potential to put a new house there. I closed on it in December.

By this time Barbie, Christina and Laurie knew all about my story. I had come to realize that the downtown bartenders — a tourist town like Sonora had about ten bars along the main drag — formed their own little social club, and were the main source of news and gossip around town. I got to know Lisa, Wendy, and Kris as well.

In February, Laurie nervously approached me and said, "I have this friend I think you might like." By now I was regularly spending weekends at the house, and so it was easier for me to be available. This friend, it seemed, was from Sonora and attended Stanislaus State University. All we needed was a weekend when she would be home.

A Saturday evening in March found me venturing beyond my usual haunts in downtown Sonora, to Wilma's Flying Pig Saloon, for a blind date with Karen. The Pig is one of those wonderful, funky old bars — dim lights, crowded tables, and an Escher-like tile pattern in the restroom of interlocking geese and winged pigs. Most weekends they feature live music, and on this night they had the Daniel Castro Band, a regional favorite on the blues scene.

Lisa — Laurie's co-conspirator in setting up this date — was tending bar, and Karen was sitting at the bar talking with her when I came in. Awkwardly, I introduced myself and sat down. We tried to talk a bit, but the band was loud, and the crowd rowdy.

After a couple of songs Karen leaned over and said, "Would you like to dance?"

Reflexively I shook my head. Like most men, I felt self conscious on the dance floor. I don't have much rhythm, and moving my hips does not come naturally. Frankly, I was always a bit envious of the easy freedom so many women find in dance.

As I looked away, Karen threw a pouting frown at Lisa, who mouthed the words, "What's wrong?"

Again, Karen leaned over. "Are you sure?"

I hesitated only for a moment. I was immediately attracted to Karen, and even with what little conversation we'd been able to manage, I found her easy to talk to. I wanted this to be an enjoyable evening, and there was only one way for that to happen. I gave a small shrug, said, "Okay," and led her out onto the dance floor.

However uncomfortable I felt at first, I soon relaxed. Karen was a natural dancer. She had an easy sway to her hips, and every step and turn she took made the curves of her body look all the more appealing. Not even I could stay uptight in the aura of all that.

We had a good time, but at the end of the evening I still felt like we were two strangers.

Our next date, what we really now think of as our first date, was an intimate dinner at the Josephine Room across the street from The Pig. I learned that Karen had gone immediately from high school to work, as a bank teller. After ten years in banking she had decided to go to college, and was in her last semester towards a degree in early childhood education.

We talked and talked, through dinner and dessert. The conversation flowed effortlessly, and I had that sensation of the entire room just disappearing except for the two of us, gazing into each other's eyes. Karen asked if I wanted to go across the street to The Pig after dinner, and I readily agreed. We stepped out into the frosty night, ice and slush everywhere. As we picked our way across the street, she grabbed my arm to steady herself, and the sensation felt electric. Somehow I just knew. We both did. We were falling in love.

Four months later I asked her to marry me, and eleven months after that we were married in a joyous ceremony in her parents' back yard, followed by a night of dinner and dancing with friends and family at the Opera Hall in downtown Sonora.

So there we were, on a cold night in December of 2005, hosting dinner for Karen's parents at our house — a proper three section modular we'd had put in on the property. Karen was very pregnant, her due date a little over two weeks away. Karen picked at her food, hardly eating, and I saw a twinge of pain pass over her face. When I looked at her inquiringly, she said, "Just cramps, I'm sure."

By 2:00 AM we knew it was not cramps. Sixteen days early, but the time had come. Nathan was born at the hospital in downtown Sonora a few hours later. Those first few moments were tearful and joyous, everything new parents expect. Karen was happy, but exhausted from a difficult breech birth that had come on so fast at the hospital that they'd had no time for any kind of pain relief.

About a half hour later the mood in the hospital room changed. The staff suddenly seemed anxious. The doctor came over to talk with us, and said,

"We're concerned about your son's blood sugar levels. We want to run some tests, but in my experience he has probably developed a respiratory infection."

By mid afternoon the doctor was sure. He was very careful to convey to us that the infection was manageable, but that Nathan would be better off in a more complete medical facility than the local hospital in Sonora could provide. They were arranging ambulance transport for Nathan to be moved to the Neonatal Intensive Care Unit (NICU) at the hospital in Modesto. At the same time, Karen would not be discharged from the hospital until the next day. Deeply distraught, she and I talked about what to do. I didn't want to leave her alone in the hospital, but we agreed that we absolutely had to have one of us at the hospital in Modesto in case there were medical decisions to be made.

The ambulance didn't arrive in Sonora until evening. I said my goodbyes to Karen, got in the car, and headed for Modesto. I struggled through the fog, the dark, my exhaustion, and that feeling of helplessness that no parent wants to experience.

The next eleven days were hard. Karen arrived in Modesto the next day, and I felt awful for her especially. Nathan was in his own little bed in the NICU, on oxygen and an IV. While we could hold him for a few minutes now and then, Karen was being denied so much of those early bonding moments that mother and child require. For days the prospects seemed unclear. Nathan had jaundice — common with premature babies — and an infection. The jaundice cleared up quickly enough, but the infection was stubborn, not getting worse but not getting better either.

For me the NICU was a lesson in humble gratitude. The nurses were so kind to us, the doctors so diligent. As concerned as we were about Nathan, we recognized that we were the lucky ones. Many babies in the NICU were months premature, not just weeks. Many had more severe conditions than an infection treatable by antibiotics.

One morning the doctor came to talk with us. He said that Nathan seemed to be responding well to the antibiotics. He didn't need to be on oxygen anymore. His blood sugar level had improved, but not to where the doctors wanted it to be.

The doctor paused, looked out the window, turned back to us and then said, "I'm confident in the days ahead his blood sugar will resolve itself. What I'm concerned about is the risk, however slight, of a sudden drop in blood sugar. It's New Year's Eve. He should be at home with his family. If you can commit to testing his blood sugar yourselves every four hours — you'll have to draw a little blood to do that — then I'd like to release him today so you can all go home."

At home the next morning, the bright, crisp, winter sunlight streamed through our picture windows to where we had Nathan's baby blanket laid out on the floor. He lay there, for the moment sleeping quietly. Fred, our cat, wandering over from where he'd been curled up in front of the wood stove, sniffed him curiously. I held Karen's hand and we looked at each other, looked at Nathan, smiled, and began to relax.

A new day. A new year. New beginnings for a new family. We had no idea of the challenges and triumphs that lay in our future. But we had each other. And we knew that would be enough.

CHAPTER 16

THE SURGEONS

February 2007 | Sonora, California

I know how fortunate I am to have Dr. Booth as a surgeon. Finding a world class surgeon outside of a major urban area is rare, and it is pure luck that he has a vacation home here in Sonora in Apple Valley, and thus maintains a limited practice in the area.

Now, almost a year after he has performed disk fusion surgery on my L5-S1 vertebrae, we sit down for what will be my final consultation with him. He's showing me the latest x-ray of my back. While the area in question is not quite shaped like the other disks, there's clearly a lot of healthy bone tissue that has filled in. Immediately after surgery the first x-ray showed only a small, I-shaped piece of plastic anchored with screws to the surrounding vertebrae. Over the intervening months, like watching coral grow around a shipwreck, I have seen more and more bone tissue fill in.

"So," I say, "You said I could expect a full recovery."

"That's right," says Dr. Booth. "Perhaps some limitations in your range of motion, but barely noticeable."

"So full exercise would be okay?"

He smiles. "It would be good for you."

I start naming off activities. "Hiking?"

"Sure."

"Bicycling?"

"Yes."

"Tennis?"

"Yes."

"Running?"

A long, quiet pause fills the room. With a small sigh, Dr. Booth says, "Well, I can't recommend it."

March 2006
Sonora, California

Outside a heavy snow tumbled through the morning sky, piling onto the previous night's blizzard. Somewhere in the room I heard screaming. It took me a long moment to realize that the screaming was my own. I had retreated to a corner of my mind as far from feeling and sensation as I could get, recoiling from that unrelenting sensation, like a burning knife, running up and down my right leg from hip to toe. That's the sensation you feel when your L5 disk has completely given way, and there's nothing left to shield your sciatic nerve from the weight of your own body.

When the paramedic came through the door, it took all the effort I had left in me to grit my teeth, stop screaming, listen to him, and try to respond.

"Sir, can you walk?"

"No."

"Can you stand?"

"No."

"Which leg?"

"Right."

"Can you feel your toes?"

"Mostly. Not the last two."

"The ambulance can't get through the snow to make it up the hill. They're chaining up, and they'll be here as soon as they can."

Twenty minutes later, feeling the sweet relief of morphine finally administered, I was carried out of my own house on a stretcher. I didn't know if I'd ever be able to walk again. I didn't know how much better my back would ever get. Yet I felt oddly calm. This was the low point of a long, long decline that had started with my first back injury almost ten years earlier. Whatever the future held, it wasn't going to get worse than this moment. Things could only get better.

It's worth noting that, at the time, we lived on the border of Stanislaus National Forest, at the end of what was classified as a "county unmaintained road". Remote doesn't begin to describe it. It's also worth saying that my wife Karen is the most amazing, heroic woman I have known. Snowed in from a blizzard, with four month old baby Nathan in her arms, far from any help, she responded to my accident magnificently. Every call that had to be made, every conversation with a doctor or paramedic or surgeon, she was right there to see that I got what I needed.

April 1997
Bear Valley, California

Spring thaw is coming, and ski areas like Bear Valley won't be open many more weekends. Today has been gorgeous, though. With the sun shining, and high temperatures in the mid-40s, I've spent most of the afternoon cross country skiing in short sleeves.

The sun is low on the horizon as I tackle a more technical trail in the back of the park. The temperature is starting to drop, and I feel the cold any time I stop moving. I'm feeling clumsy on a course that is clearly over my ability level. Since I did not even take up skiing until my mid-20s, I'll never be graceful at it. But like most athletic endeavors I undertake, what I lack in ability, I make up for in enthusiasm.

I've slogged my way to the top of the main hill on this trail, and now it's just a winding series of small downhills back to the parking lot a couple of miles north. Biting down on my heels with as much force as I can, I snowplow my way through a few turns. Coming around a tight corner the slope drops away more than I expected, and I realize that the day's thaw is beginning to freeze over. I'm way off center as I try to get my skis under me. In a split second my feet fly out from under me to the front, and I am airborne looking up at the trees. With an audible "whump" I land on a flat, icy patch, the small of my back taking the full weight of my fall.

Slowly, gingerly, I get up. I clip back in to my skis, and shuffle back towards the parking lot. But something is clearly not right. There's a searing, burning pain in my lower back, and it stays with me all the way on the long drive back to the San Francisco Bay area. It will be six months before I heed the pain enough to go see a doctor, and 18 months beyond that before they reach a diagnosis — herniated disk. And that diagnosis is not the end. It is only the beginning. The beginning of years and years in which I'll go through two surgeries, and lose my active lifestyle in an effort to shelter my fragile spine.

I lost a decade to that injury.

September 1999
San Francisco

Immediately after the injury I went through 18 months of trying various physical therapy approaches as well as cortisone injections. None of this provided long term relief, and indeed my condition worsened. At that point the only real option was surgery. In September of 1999 I had a laminectomy performed.

Dr. Zukerman, my surgeon, was great. He explained that the procedure would not resolve the problem, but would relieve the symptoms. I had a ruptured disk, and the tissue that had been squeezed out of that rupture was pressing against my sciatic nerve. He would remove the tissue, but would not attempt anything to repair the disk.

His reasons were very clear. At that time procedures like disk fusion were highly invasive, far from 100% successful, and required a lengthy rehabilitation. What he was proposing would instead provide relief for a long time, perhaps as much as ten years, which would give time for the technology of more reconstructive surgeries to improve dramatically. Do the least necessary to relieve the problem, and play for time. That was his recommendation.

I agreed. There was one important caveat, however. After the surgery I would still have a ruptured disk, which I would have to handle gingerly. Strenuous physical activity, particularly high impact activities like running, were out of the question.

Post surgery, I mostly abided by his restrictions. I played tennis once in a while, and the occasional pick-up game of basketball. Our home up in the Sierra Nevadas was on five and a half acres of gorgeous pine forest. One of my favorite activities was splitting firewood to lay in for our wood stove over the winter. After a really good snow fall I could cross country ski right out my front door.

Mostly though, I led a less active life than I had before. That and middle age took a toll, and I put on weight. Even a vigorous hike left me short of breath, particularly up in the thin mountain air.

Then in 2006 I was struck by the event that Dr. Zukerman foretold. The ambulance ride to the hospital that led me to the skilled hands of Dr. Booth.

In the months that followed I gradually resumed physical activity, and progress was rapid. In many respects I resumed a more active lifestyle than I had known in years. Still, I abided by my surgeon's advice and stayed away from running.

By January 2009 I was ready to risk it. Almost three years had passed since the surgery. I was 49 years old, and as I thought about my pending 50th birthday, I felt the need to do something. I was 40 pounds over my pre-back injury weight, and feeling defeated by middle age. And nothing motivates me like running. I figured if I felt any real back pain or discomfort at all I could back off and try some other form of exercise. But I might as well start with what I loved the most.

CHAPTER 17

CAPITAL CITY MARATHON

June 2014 | Olympia, Washington

"The marathon is less a physical event than a spiritual encounter. In infinite wisdom, God built into us a 32-km racing limit, a limit imposed by inadequate sources of the marathoner's prime racing fuel — carbohydrates. But we, in our human wisdom, decreed that the standard marathon be raced over 42 km. So it is in that physical no-man's-land, which begins after the 32-km mark, that the irresistible appeal of the marathon lies."

— *Dr. Timothy Noakes, in "The Lore of Running"*

Let me start by talking about mile 18. By Tim Noakes's narrative, it is just beyond the 18th mile that we reach the climax of a story that we hope will have positive resolution at mile 26.2. At this point I've run three marathons. To me, mile 18 is the most revealing.

The 2012 Seattle Marathon was my first, and I reached mile 18 in 3 hours flat. But by that time I was already desperate. My left hamstring had cramped at mile 14, and would not relinquish until mile 22. By then I was on the edge of hypothermia from a combination of damp, cold air and sheer fatigue. I finished in 4 hours, 50 minutes, meaning it took me almost 2 hours to finish the last eight miles.

For the Winthrop Marathon in 2013 I was better prepared, both mentally and physically. I hit mile 18 in 3 hours and 5 minutes, and felt in control rather than desperate. But I had benefited from 1500 feet of elevation drop to that point, as well as running in the cool shade of Okanogan National Forest. What lay before me was 8 miles of unrelenting sun, with temperatures rising to 80, across elevation-neutral terrain of rolling hills. I finished in 4 hours, 54 minutes, requiring the same time as Seattle to traverse the last 8 miles.

Which brings me to the present, and the Capital City Marathon in Olympia, Washington. No sub-40 degree temperatures like Seattle. No 70+ degree temperatures like Winthrop. And no eager start foolishly burning fuel I would need down the stretch. I crossed mile 18 in 3 hours 6 minutes and 30 seconds, my slowest start to date. With a PR finish time of 4 hours 46 minutes and 17 seconds, that means I completed those final 8.2 miles almost 10 minutes faster than my previous two marathons.

My fastest mile? Mile 14, at 9:40. My second fastest mile? Mile 18, at 9:46. Is there room for improvement? Yes. But this was a vastly better pacing effort on my part than either of my previous marathon efforts.

Olympia sits at the very southern end of the Puget Sound, and the Olympia waterfront is built along Budd Inlet. The course wanders along or close to the eastern shore of Budd Inlet before climbing inland to follow the ridgeline back into town. There's a big dip just as you come back into Olympia, and then a commensurate climb that stretches through miles 22 and 23 before you turn towards the capitol building for a flat mile 24 and then a gentle downhill to the finish line. The long out and back along Budd Inlet crosses a number of small streams tumbling towards the inlet, and these create the defining terrain of the race. While not a hilly course overall — the highest point on the course is only about 200 feet above the lowest point — there are a half dozen or so big dips where the course drops 75-100 feet to cross one of these stream beds and then quickly climbs back up the other side. These steep descents and ascents, repeated over and over, make the course more challenging than your typical "flat" course.

Part of the appeal of the Capital City Marathon is the weather. Mid-May in Olympia is guaranteed to be just about perfect. This year the start time temperature was 50, the finish line temperature was about 65, most of the race was sunny, and just when the sun was threatening to yield real heat, the clouds rolled in.

And I love how Olympia blends the elements of an urban road race with the intimacy of a smaller event. Residents of Olympia really do come out in numbers to cheer the runners on, from the folks blasting "Staying Alive" out of the back of their SUV to the gal holding up the "Pain now, beer later" sign, to the couple offering Fireball on the rocks at about mile 23. Not a huge crowd, but a fun and enthusiastic crowd. The marathon only has about 300 runners, so when you cross the finish line the announcer has time to call out your name, number, and the town you're from. That's a refreshing change from a big race where you get quickly herded through, handed your medal, and then hastily shunted off to the side to make way for other runners.

Finally a note on history. Olympia is not an obvious place to host a 30+ year old marathon, but there's a story. Local resident Angela French was a promising marathon runner who had Olympic aspirations when it was announced that the 1984 Los Angeles Games would be the first to have a Women's Marathon. One question: where to hold the Olympic Trials to determine who would represent the U.S. in that first Women's Marathon? In part to support French, Olympia submitted and won a bid to be the host city for the trials, and so the Capital City Marathon was born. This year, 2014, the 30th anniversary of the Los Angeles Games, Ms. French was there at the starting line to tell her story and call the start of the race.

So, what was my game plan? In order to avoid starting too fast, and to spread my effort more evenly over the whole race, I opted for a modified Galloway "run-walk" approach. The plan was:

- Run the first three miles at a 10:30 pace;
- Walk two minutes;
- Run two miles at 9:45 pace;
- Walk two minutes;
- Repeat the previous two steps for as long as I could sustain it;

- Switch to one mile run, two minute walk if necessary;
- Reduce running pace if necessary.

My primary goal was not a time goal. My primary goal was to run a controlled race where I could finish feeling I had made a complete effort but where I had not suffered to the point of distress. Neither of my previous two marathons met that goal. In terms of pace, if the 9:45 run, two minute walk was sustainable start to finish, I would end up with a time of 4 hours 30 minutes. However, I was completely prepared to back off that pace depending on how I felt.

I'll note this was also my first marathon wearing a GPS watch, and none of this careful planning would have been possible to execute without a good watch to track my progress.

Finally, fuel and fluids: in a reversal of my previous approaches, I planned to hit every aid station for water and/or energy drink. It would help me stay hydrated, and help me keep my pace from creeping up. I also wore my fuel belt with a 10 ounce bottle of water and a 10 ounce bottle of Gatorade. For miles 10, 15, and 20 I had three packets wrapped up with a mix of banana chips, candy corn, almonds, and chocolate covered espresso beans. This part of my plan I was completely satisfied with. For a future race in similar temperature conditions, I wouldn't change a thing.

Holding back from a fast start is so hard. The crowd is there, all the runners are together, and your energy is at a peak from the combination of training and taper. My efforts to hold back were more successful this time, and I found I actually liked the run-walk rhythm.

Through the first 10 miles I found myself catching up to and then dropping back from the 4:30 pace runner as I switched from run to walk. We chatted quite a bit through this stretch. He was a hard core ultra runner out for the day combining a bit of volunteering with what was for him an easy training run. We compared notes on local routes and races, and he really gave me confidence that I could aspire to an ultra.

After mile 10 we fell out of sync, and I could see him up ahead for awhile but I didn't catch up to him again. The next six miles were the hardest mentally. At this point you've left Olympia behind and you're out in the countryside. The landscape offers up lush hills and quiet creeks emptying into Puget Sound, but the crowds are gone. And the runners are all spread out, so there were long stretches with no other runner nearby. This is also the stretch in which most of those steep "dips" occur. While I like to let the throttle out on the downhills and give my long legs a chance to stretch, by the time I hit mile 16 I could tell that the pounding on the downhills was beginning to take a toll.

Then along came Breezy (yes, that's what she said her name was). Purple spandex, pony tail flying, she passed me and said, "Tag, you're it!" Chicked again. About a half mile later I caught up to her. "I've been chasing you for miles," she said. Turns out this was her first marathon, and she was clearly having the time of her life. And she certainly lifted my spirits too. Even as she left me behind.

My two mile run, two minute walk pattern held up well until mile 19. At that point my legs were starting to feel heavy, and my glutes were burning from the pounding on those steep downhills. My pace had begun to slow, but not by much. Through the early miles I was maintaining 10:17 per mile, which is really a tad faster than I intended. By mile 19 I had slowed to 10:35, a little off where I hoped to be but still in line with the plan. Easing up to save something for the end seemed prudent.

About this time I caught up with Jeff. Built like a fire hydrant, and pigeon-toed giving him the look of a duck waddling when he ran, He kept slapping out strides, but was clearly struggling. He, too, was a first time marathon runner and we ran together for a bit. I told him he should feel proud, because he was absolutely going to finish even if he had to walk the last miles to the finish line. That really did cheer him up.

We were now entering mile 23, and the start of the long, last hill. At this point many more runners were walking than actually running. I continued shuffling forward at a slow jog, all thought of pace and run-walk rhythm now gone. I would jog as much as I could, and walk the rest. I was dimly aware that I had once again hit "the Wall", the point at which my body could no longer draw on carbohydrate reserves. My previous journeys into this realm had left me defeated both mentally and physically, essentially unable to run. This time around I knew I was struggling, but I wasn't suffering. I kept jogging.

Jeff fell behind. I passed a few more runners. Then that blaze of purple; I caught up to and passed Breezy. "Tag, you're it" I called as I went by. She looked up and managed to turn a grimace into a smile, nodding in my direction. Then it was my turn to walk. Breezy passed me back, now jogging herself. I would not catch up to her again.

Jeff pulled up even with me again. "How much more of this hill is there?" He had a note of desperation in his voice. I did him the kindest favor I could think of. I lied. "Oh, we're just about halfway." It looked to me like we'd covered about a half mile of the two mile hill, but he didn't need to know that. We passed each other back and forth, depending on which of us was walking or jogging.

I walked the last 200 yards or so up that hill, reaching the "Mile 24" sign. Though the course flattened out, I was having a tough time pushing myself to start running again. Then the 4:45 pace runner passed me, the first pace runner I'd seen since Mile 10. The pacer passed Jeff just ahead of me, and that seemed to rouse him. They ran side by side, the pacer talking him through it, the rest of the way.

It was all the motivation I needed too. I had hit the Wall. But for the first time in a marathon, I had pushed through it. And I could run again. More slowly to be sure, but I kept Jeff and the pace runner in sight. I felt empty, spent, but not in distress. Somehow the ability to keep running was still there. The flat course turned to a gradual downhill, the road widened, and the crowd grew. I could see the finish line as we passed the park in front of the capitol building. I heard the announcer calling out my name, and I saw and then heard Karen and Nathan cheering for me. With a smile that grew with each stride, I crossed the finish line.

The Capital City Marathon taught me a lot. I learned that I can run a controlled marathon, start to finish. I learned I could encounter the Wall and break through. But I also learned that, given my current approach to training and running, I would hit the Wall. And I had to think about that.

In the past 15 months, I'd set PRs at every distance I raced: 10K, half marathon, and marathon. To do that I'd run almost 2000 training miles; it isn't easy to get faster as you become older. Unless I changed something fundamental, I could not expect to improve much further in the marathon. Perhaps the answer was to run farther, not faster. Gorges Waterfalls 50K in 2015 loomed as a very tempting first ultra.

Yet surely there would be a next marathon somewhere in my future. Because somewhere after the 32-km mark, the irresistible appeal of the marathon still calls.

CHAPTER 18

RUNNER REBORN

February 2009 | Buckley, Washington

I began the first week of February. On the first day out I covered a mile and a half at a slow jog, and I had to stop twice to catch my breath. I kept at it, running every other day. My back never gave me any trouble.

My route took me on a trail through the woods behind our house, across the grounds of the high school, and up the road on the other side. Each day I'd reach a particular telephone pole, turn around, and return. Each week I'd pick a new telephone pole further up the street as my destination. After a couple of months I reached the traffic light at the end of the road; my distance had grown to three miles.

Soon three miles became five miles. In our garage we had a treadmill that had been sitting idle. I dusted it off, and on days when the weather was bad — we have a few of those in the Pacific Northwest — I ran on the treadmill. I kept adding mileage. In my youth I don't think I had ever run farther than seven miles. Back then five miles felt like a "long" run. Now I routinely had at least one eight-mile run a week.

I had not participated in an organized sporting event since high school, so I'm not sure what inspired me to sign up for my first race as an adult. I have always been a solitary runner. Running for me is quiet, meditative, a time for looking inward. Yet I knew I had accomplished something very important for me. Perhaps it was just a need to mark the event symbolically.

In May of 2012 I found myself in Gas Works Park in Seattle, lining up at the starting line for the Seattle 15K. A typical Pacific Northwest light rain fell, but the temperature was in the 50s, and overall it was a great day for running. At roughly 2000 runners, this was a mid-sized event. I, however, had never taken part in anything like this before, and I found the crowd and the excitement intoxicating. The course is beautiful, a real showcase for Seattle. You head west out of Gas Works Park, through the trendy Fremont neighborhood, and then south across the Fremont Bridge. Turning west again there's an out and back along the ship canal, the narrow passage of water that connects Lake Washington to the east with Elliott Bay and Puget Sound to the west. After the ship canal leg the course follows the perimeter of Lake Union before a steep climb up to and over the East Lake Bridge and a home stretch leg along Burke-Gilman Trail and back into Gas Works Park.

My longest training run had been eight miles. Buoyed by the vibe from all the other runners, I cruised through the first six miles effortlessly. While I started to feel the strain around Mile 7, my pace didn't let up. Then just after Mile 8 I hit the big hill up to the East Lake Bridge. My pace dropped precipitously, but I never slowed to a walk. I propelled myself forward with a simple mantra: "With each stride I am running farther than I have ever run before."

My finishing time was 1:25:13, good for a pace of 9:08 minutes per mile. I was thrilled, and I was hooked. Over the next year I would run a 10K, two half marathons, and sign up for my first marathon, the fateful 2012 Seattle Marathon.

Up through the completion of my first half marathon, I did not run with any real training plan. I ran every other day, and I tried to have one run on the weekend where I emphasized distance over speed, and one run during the week where I focused on speed but tried to maintain a reasonable distance (about five miles). However, I didn't feel my first half marathon attempt was really successful, and I realized if I was going to push myself to those distances that I had to get serious and organized about training.

I don't know what runners did before the Internet. These days, however, there are as many training plans, and as many assessments of training plans online as one has time for. For my purposes, I made some small modifications to a Galloway beginner's marathon plan and settled in on that.

My plan consisted of three days a week of running, and one day a week of cross training:

- Long slow run: slower than race pace, focused on building stamina and time on feet. For a half marathon I peaked at 15 miles, and for the Seattle Marathon I worked up to two long runs of 18 miles and two long runs of 20 miles.

- Tempo run: Shorter run intended to be at race pace or a little faster, but shorter than race distance. This helps build speed, but mainly helps acclimate to running the desired pace. For a half marathon I worked up to eight miles at about 8:30 per mile pace, and for the Seattle Marathon I worked up to ten miles at 9:30 per mile pace.

- Interval run: Intervals can be done in many different ways. The goal is to focus on speed as a way of building strength and increasing speed. I ran on the treadmill in our garage. I would do a quarter mile working up to ten MPH, holding that for 60 seconds, and easing back down. Then I would jog for two minutes. Then I would run at an 8% incline, working up to eight MPH, holding that for 30 seconds, and easing back down, followed by another two minute jog. That cycle was what I called one interval. I would start out doing three sets of these, and by the end of my training cycle I would be doing six sets.

- Cross training: 45 minutes of some low impact form of exercise other than running. I did walking, cycling, and swimming at various times.

This approach works out to a peak weekly mileage of about 35 miles when training for a marathon. The plan is workable — I did finish the Seattle Marathon, and training wasn't really my shortcoming — but it's minimal. To really be set up for success, a marathon plan should include at least four days a week of running, a peak weekly mileage of at least 40 miles, and some strength training as well.

CHAPTER 19

RUN FOR JACOBY

August 2014 | Bonney Lake, Washington

Nathan is nine years old, and for five years he has watched me turn in mile after mile of training runs. He has stood at the finish line for my joyful finish in the Capital City Half Marathon, and for my grueling finish at the Winthrop Marathon. Now he and I are toeing the starting line together for a 5K, his first race.

Running events and charity have always had a close relationship. Many races have a way for participants to contribute to a worthy cause, and some races are entirely dedicated to a cause. Jacoby Miles is a young woman and former gymnast in the neighboring town of Bonney Lake. A tragic training accident left her with a broken neck and paralysis from the chest down. Like many families beset by sudden tragedy, the Miles family were unprepared for the financial burden of Jacoby's ongoing therapy and medical treatment. Friends and family organized the annual Run for Jacoby race to raise funds to help out. Charity begins at home, and the opportunity to contribute to a local cause was compelling.

This all started four months earlier. It was a Saturday morning. I had just returned from my weekly long run as I was training for the Capital City Marathon. Nervously, Nathan approached me as I was in the kitchen getting water, and said, "Dad, can I go running with you some time?"

My heart soared. When Nathan was younger, Karen and I had tried him out in a couple of sports — first gymnastics, and later soccer. He was unhappy with both, and we resolved not to push him any further in the direction of organized sports. While I would never have pushed Nathan to try running, a father can't help but hope that his son will want to share an athletic activity with him.

It's three quarters of a mile from our house to the high school, and so we start out running in the neighborhood, once or twice a week, over to the high school and back. Nathan has all the usual beginner's complaints: "This is uncomfortable." "I'm out of breath." "I have a stitch in my side." But he sticks with it. There's a lot of walking — sometimes as much walking as running — but after a few weeks it's clear that he's going to see this through, and so I search out local 5K races, finding and registering us for the Run for Jacoby.

By early summer I can see that Nathan is not developing much stamina, and that he's struggling with road running; fighting the run more than letting the run come to him. On a whim, I take him with me up to Mount Rainier one Sunday morning, up to Mowich Lake. Several trails pass through here, and I pick an easy route for us. Ipsut Pass is about a mile from the Mowich Lake, the trail following gently rolling ups and downs through the forest before emerging with a spectacular panoramic view of the valley through which Ipsut Creek descends, merging with the Carbon River some 3000 feet below and three miles ahead.

The quiet of the forest, and the sound of a gentle breeze whispering through the mountains, has a calming effect on Nathan. I can see him relax as he runs. The narrow, winding trail with the occasional root or rock protruding also forces him to shorten his stride, and to focus on it. We complete a two mile out and back more easily, and also faster, than any of the neighborhood runs we've done up to this point.

In the weekends ahead we extend this route to Eunice Lake, and we tackle the more ambitious trail out to Spray Falls. That's a five mile round trip with over 1600 feet of elevation gain. On the outbound leg, Nathan catches his toe on a root and falls hard. Immediately he bursts into tears, but I can see that he is more startled than hurt. I chuckle, and say, "Face plant! You're a trail runner for sure now." He wipes the tears aside, manages a grin, and says, "Trail runner. Yeah."

The trail is gorgeous, and worth the effort. A short descent from Mowich Lake joins with the Wonderland Trail, which runs out on the shoulder of a ridge, and then turns to a steep ascent. After the ascent a short side trail takes you over to Eagle Cliff, a high overlook with a view of Spray Creek far below, and the beginnings of the Rainier snow cap across the valley and up the slope. Spray Falls is at the base of another steep ascent — which we do not undertake — that leads up to Spray Park, a spectacular high alpine meadow rich with wildflowers in the late summer. A short way from the falls is Eagle's Roost, a backcountry campsite.

Nathan eyes the handful of tents and the backpackers sorting their gear, and says, "We should camp here some time."

We have done father-son camping trips since before Nathan could talk, but I have never yet taken him backpacking. I look at him thoughtfully. He is growing, and changing.

By the time August rolls around, Nathan is ready for his 5K. While he hasn't gotten any faster, he has some stamina now, and should be able to handle three miles comfortably. And so we find ourselves at Allan Yorke Park, on the shore of Lake Tapps. There's a good sized crowd, the atmosphere is festive, and we have about 200 runners ready to go.

We line up close to the front of the pack, since most of the participants are walkers. As we settle in to wait for the start, the local cross country team trots up — each one lanky and energetic in a way I can still remember from decades ago. An air horn signals the start, and Nathan takes off with every intent of keeping up with the cross country guys. I call after him, "Hold on there, tiger! Let's pace ourselves a little bit." Reluctantly he slows back down, and we settle into a more reasonable pace.

About five minutes into the race, a young boy — he couldn't have been more than seven — passes us, running all by himself, no parent in sight. A determined look spreads from Nathan's jaw across his face, and he picks up the pace to move back ahead of the boy. We're going a bit faster than our training runs warrant, but I smile and indulge him. Every minute or so

Nathan looks back over his shoulder to make sure we're still in the lead, and after a few minutes the lad slows down, and disappears somewhere amongst the runners and walkers behind us.

Now we turn away from Lake Tapps, following surface streets through the neighborhood that will wind back to our starting point. This part of the course is more challenging, with rolling hills rather than the flat, straight course by the waterfront. By the time we hit Mile 2, we begin to experience a smaller version of what every distance runner knows from long races — the runners are all spread out now, with almost everyone in front of us moving faster than us, and everyone behind moving slower, so that the distance between us and other runners increases. This creates the impression that we're running alone.

Nathan, feeling uneasy, says, "Where is everyone?"

I reply, "Don't worry about it. We're more than halfway."

Nathan's aggressive early pace, and the hillier course, take a toll, and we start to slow for walking breaks every few minutes. I let him take his time.

As we approach 2.75 miles, I see the course marker for our last turn, taking us onto the road to the lake down a long, straight stretch with gradual downhill. I nudge Nathan back to a run, and he grumbles, "This is so far! When will we be done?" Then we turn the corner, and he can see the banner above the finish line, and the crowd of waiting spectators. He moves more steadily now, extending his stride and picking up the pace. I can see Karen waiting, and Nathan sees her too. With a final burst he sprints across the finish line, and into his mother's arms.

"You did it," she beams. "I'm so proud of you."

CHAPTER 20

EVERYBODY RUNS FOR SOMEONE

May 2013 | Buckley, Washington

One of the particularities of the running community is the degree to which we use the challenges of others to motivate ourselves. This relationship is most clearly institutionalized in the Susan G. Komen Foundation's ongoing "Race for the Cure" endeavor. The "Race for the Cure" series started as a single event in 1983 and has grown to a series of 150 races a year with more than 1.5 million participants.

Inspiration for many runners is intensely personal: the father-son Team Hoyt has become a fixture at the Boston Marathon. The son, Rick, suffers from cerebral palsy, is wheelchair bound, and requires computer assistance in order to communicate. Father Dick pushes his son in a wheelchair so they can participate in marathons together. They have participated in more than 70 marathons and completed the Boston Marathon.

My own source of inspiration is more modest, and very personal. As I trained for the Winthrop Marathon, Karen and I were coming up on our 11th wedding anniversary, which would be in June, just a couple of weeks after the marathon.

Karen is a lively, active person. She loves to dance. She loves to incorporate dance into her own fitness routine. Here in the rainy Pacific Northwest she fills the weekends when the sun graces us with its presence by asking, "What can we do outside?" She has also battled health and weight issues her entire life.

These issues are not of her own making and thus, sadly, she is limited in what she can do to battle them. The symptoms are numerous, but the pattern is generally what the medical profession labels as autoimmune disorders: her metabolism sabotaging her, her body attacking itself.

We hit a personal low point in the Spring of 2012 when she found a lump in the salivary gland on the right side of her face. An anxious couple of weeks followed, in which we learned far more than I ever wanted to know about lymphoma. Then I sat through two hours of what seemed to me like the longest surgery in the world. Ultimately the news was almost entirely good. The surgeon pronounced the mass "troubling, but not cancerous." So now Karen, who remains so far unmarked by cancer, nonetheless has added an oncologist to her annual tour of specialists she must see.

Of course we were incredibly relieved with Karen's prognosis. Yet to me it underscored the depths of the struggle Karen faces. This beautiful person, who has great instincts for healthy living and a sincere desire for an active lifestyle, has to work so hard just to make modest headway against the challenges that metabolism and genetics have placed before her.

In the face of these challenges I have seen her show frustration, bitterness, despair, and even just plain grumpiness. But those instances have been rare, and have been the exception. Far more often she has been cheerful, determined, and courageous. She has come so far, healthier now than during all the time I have known her; more in command of her health than ever before. And of course to me she is more beautiful now than ever. This daily marathon of hers is far from over, but in my eyes she is winning. Nothing in life makes me more proud than what she has accomplished.

I thought about all of this when I was in the depths of suffering through the Seattle Marathon. I hated that I was suffering. I didn't want to give up. And the thought I kept returning to was this: "Everything Karen tries to do is harder than anything I try to do. If she can remain determined, then so can I." A marathon involves months of training, but not more than that. The race itself is over, one way or another, in a matter of hours. But in the quest for good health, Karen's marathon is never-ending. It will last a lifetime.

The following spring, as the weeks rolled by in my Winthrop Marathon training, as I pushed my way in solitude up and down the slopes of Mount Rainier, I thought about all of this. Deep inside, in those quiet and most honest moments, I recognized a small bit of selfishness. I liked to tell myself that Karen needed me to be as determined a runner as I was, because my discipline would inspire and comfort her in her own challenges. Yet honestly those thoughts do her a disservice. She is a well of strength deeper than even she realizes. She doesn't need me to be strong; it is I who need her. When it rains outside, and I lace up my shoes anyway, I need her. When my alarm goes off well before dawn and I get out of bed, I need her. When wind and cold have beaten me down to where I no longer have the desire to put one foot in front of the other, I need her. When the mental fatigue from week after week of an ever more demanding training routine sets in, I need her.

Everybody runs for someone. I run for Karen.

ICARUS

March 2015 | Benson State Park, Oregon

Never regret thy fall,
O Icarus of the fearless flight
For the greatest tragedy of them all
Is never to feel the burning light

— Oscar Wilde

As runners we thrill with each new height ascended, whether it's the first marathon completed or a new PR at a favorite distance. In that moment our emotions burn bright with the glow of achievement, and we wonder, with hope, how much higher we might ascend. We are undaunted by the risk that someday we will fall, and from a great height.

The ancient Greeks intended the tale of Icarus as a sober reminder that we are not immortals granted unbounded ascension, and thus our aspirations must be grounded in the humble bounds of what is possible for mere mortals. This we all understand when first we hear the tale of Icarus, and this lesson in humility is the origin of the expression, "Pride goeth before a fall."

I took my own great fall at the Gorge Waterfalls 50K, plummeting from more than a thousand feet above the gleaming waters of the Columbia River, and more than 24 miles out from the starting line, to the wreckage of my first "Did Not Finish" in a race. Yet in my failed attempt I was reminded of two lessons from the tale of Icarus beyond the lesson of humility, lessons that are oft forgotten in the retelling of the tale.

First, we forget that "Do not fly too close to the sun" was only one piece of advice that Daedalus gave to his son. Icarus was also advised not to fly too low, lest the dampness of the sea saturate his wings and drag him down. So in the familiar Greek manner the lesson is really about finding the happy medium — be ambitious, just not too ambitious.

I am competitive. While I do not race to win, I do race to challenge myself. Running has long since ceased to be merely about fitness and health for me, and has become a quest to push myself to new limits. A casual runner for many years, I have only gotten serious about running since I turned 50. As a "late bloomer" every PR I've run is from my fifties. And I've run it all on a crippled leg. What tantalizes me most is not how fast I can run, but how far. So an attempt at a 50K seemed like a natural next step.

Rainshadow Running's Gorge Waterfalls 50K, however, is not just any 50K. With 6000 feet of elevation gain (and descent), including a climb of 1500 feet to the last checkpoint at Mile 25.5, the course is far steeper than most ultras. The terrain is also challenging: endless miles of single track, stream crossings, scrambles across jagged moraine, tree roots waiting in ambush, and switchbacks that seem endless. Not a course for the faint of heart, and perhaps an arrogant choice for a first ultra attempt. Yet I still don't think so. In the end, I think it was just right for me. While I did not complete the course, the course completed me.

The second overlooked lesson from the tale of Icarus is "Do not fly alone." Recall that the journey of Daedalus and Icarus was an escape from imprisonment on Crete, and that Daedalus had fashioned wax and feather wings for both of them to make this escape. Because Icarus flew off on his own, no one was there to catch his fall.

What I took to heart most from the Gorge was a powerful reminder of what a welcoming community ultra runners are. No matter what your ability or what your struggle, you are never removed from their supportive embrace. Truly you are never alone.

After the previous May's Capital City Marathon, I was looking for new challenges. A summer battle with Achilles tendonitis kept me from trying anything ambitious in the Fall, but I had a growing sense that a 50K should be my next challenge. My friend Ken Ludt and I both saw the Ginger Runner's inspirational YouTube video of the 2014 Gorge Waterfalls 50K, and Ken decided he wanted to fly out from Ohio to run in the 2015 race. I couldn't have him come all the way to the Pacific Northwest alone, so I decided to join him.

There was only one catch. Gorge Waterfalls 50K is a hugely popular race. Not surprising given the size and strength of the Pacific Northwest running community, and given that the finish line is less than an hour from downtown Portland. With the stunning scenery of the Columbia Gorge (a protected National Recreation Area), and the intense challenge of the course itself, the race has international appeal. In 2015 we had runners from as far away as Marseilles and Puerto Rico. With that kind of popularity and the need to limit the entries to less than 400 runners, entry is by lottery. Unless... unless you provide a volunteer. Ken and I prevailed upon our significant others, Rose Mary and Karen, to serve as volunteers so that we could automatically gain entry. This might be the biggest spouse favor I've ever asked, but it meant the world to me to have Karen fully involved in the event with me.

This was a tough training season for me and for Ken, starting in early November and spanning the coldest and darkest months of the year. We lose daylight rapidly here in the winter months of the Pacific Northwest, so I had many long runs that started well before sunrise with only a head lamp for illumination. Rain is a constant companion this time of year; my final long training run was 6 hours and 40 minutes in a steady rain. Ken had his own challenges as Ohio suffered under one of the snowiest winters on record.

This dashed any hopes Ken had of getting in a few decent trail runs in preparation; he spent more hours than I can even imagine on the treadmill.

As the grind of training wore on, and the anticipation grew, the race crept into every nook and cranny of my thoughts. For about ten days prior to the race I had this recurring dream. In my dream Ken and I were running side by side down the final stretch, and I was encouraging him. I'd wake up, and think to myself, "How odd. I'm pretty sure that Ken is the stronger runner." The dream never made any sense. Indeed on race day I would quickly put that dream out of my thoughts. Ken did prove to be the stronger runner, and spent a lot of time that day encouraging me, for which I am eternally grateful.

Race weekend arrived. Karen and I picked up Rose Mary and Ken the afternoon before the race at the Portland airport. We had a delightful early dinner in Portland, and a quiet evening at the hotel. Rose Mary was to help with sign-ins first thing in the morning, and Karen's volunteer duties would be serving food at the finish line in the afternoon. For the 50K, runners check in at the finish area at Benson State Park, and then we are bused to the starting line at Wyeth Campground for a point to point run back to the finish.

The next morning, Rose Mary, Ken and I arrived early so that Rose Mary could get started on her volunteer assignment. In the gray pre-dawn, Ken and I strolled around the finish area, and on a whim we started walking the course backwards from the finish line. Benson State Park features a small lake, and the course winds around the far side of the lake before doubling back to the finish line. We walked all the way around the lake, and a mile or so later found ourselves at the base of Multnomah Falls, the most popular tourist destination in all of Oregon. At over 600 feet it is Oregon's tallest waterfall. We made our way back to Benson State Park. After final preparations it was time to board the buses for the starting line.

The mood on the bus was cheerful and positive. I sat next to a young man who had run eight previous ultras; this was his 3rd time at Gorge Waterfalls 50K. He was very encouraging, assuring me that I would do great. I commented that this was a big unknown for me since it was my first ultra attempt, and I didn't really know what to expect. He laughed, noting that experience wouldn't necessarily change that. Then for just a moment he got very quiet, the weight of our endeavor suddenly real to him, and said, "I don't even know what to expect today."

Start time was scheduled for 9:00 AM. Ken and I had agreed to run the race together as much as possible. We waited anxiously, and finally at 9:12, Race Director James Varner signaled the start and we were off. There are three checkpoints / aid stations on the course — at Mile 9.3, Mile 18, and Mile 25.5. Runners have 2 1/2 hours for the first two legs, and two hours for the last two legs.

The race starts immediately with a four mile run up 1000 feet of elevation gain, narrowing very quickly to single track. There's a dip of a mile or so, giving up about 200 feet in elevation, and then another steep hill. Then it's gradual downhill all the way to the first checkpoint. I took two falls in the first leg, the second including a spectacular barrel roll about 15 feet down a hillside. I suffered nothing more than a few scrapes from either, though, and entering the first checkpoint I felt good. While my intent had been to conserve energy on the first leg, Ken and I were told we were only ten minutes ahead of the cutoff time, which was cutting it closer than I had intended.

The second leg was tough, much tougher than I expected. Knowing that the third leg included the big climb of 1500 feet, and wanting to bank some time for that effort, Ken and I set out from Checkpoint 1 at a brisk pace. With the big 1000 foot climb in the first leg behind us, I was hoping for relatively easy going in the middle stretch. For a couple of miles the going was indeed easier. But of the 6000 feet of elevation gain on the course, the first and final hills make up only 2500 feet. The other 3500 feet comes from all the smaller hills in between. Hill after hill of 300 to 500 feet, with switchbacks and grades of roughly 10%, with a few spots even steeper. This kind of terrain had been a staple of my training runs, but I was now about a half marathon in and that first big climb up from the starting line had taken more out of me than I realized.

By Mile 12 I was struggling, and the next two miles were particularly difficult. It was obvious that while Ken had not put in the trail miles I had, his extensive time at steep inclines on the treadmill was paying off. He was powering up hills that I was struggling up. And I just could not find a comfortable rhythm. Everything I tried felt either too fast or too slow. Then we caught up with two women running in tandem down the single track ahead of us. Silently we fell in behind them. Nobody said a word. Yet the woman in the lead of our little group had found the groove. Her pace was perfect, and the rest of us just followed her all the way into Checkpoint 2.

I had a drop bag waiting for me, enabling me to swap into lighter and drier clothing, and leave behind the jacket and long sleeve shirt I no longer needed. While I was changing one of the volunteers refilled the water in my fuel pack. Mentally, I was struggling. I kept thinking that we still had a half marathon to go, including the biggest climb yet on the course. A quick time check showed us coming up on 2:00, right at the cut off time. That was discouraging. We had hoped to bank time on this leg, and instead had lost a little bit of time. It dawned on me that though I might have the strength to reach Checkpoint 3, time might well run out on me.

Somewhere in the background I heard one of the volunteers calling out to the runners, "You have time. You have until 4:12 at the next checkpoint." However, I was so focused on my run that I didn't really process what she was saying. Elsewhere I heard a couple of other volunteers making arrangements to drive some runners back who were dropping out, and I realized in a few minutes more they would start pulling runners from the course for missing the cutoff time. I looked at Ken as he shouldered his refilled fuel pack. He was clearly feeling fresher than me, and I was holding him back. The next cutoff time at Checkpoint 3 was going to be a very near thing. At that moment it would have been easy to drop out, and it was so tempting. This was a low point, a moment when my dampened wings nearly dragged me down. But somewhere inside of me a little voice said, "No. It doesn't end here. You have to see what you have left."

I looked again at Ken. If today I was to be Icarus, then I would follow my Daedalus. "Let's go," I said.

So began the third leg.

At first I was just walking. But this stretch was flat, following a road, and I told myself that if I wanted a chance at making the cutoff time I had to at least jog the relatively easy stretches. So after a couple hundred yards I started running, slowly. Ken was running in front of me. He looked over his shoulder, smiling and offering words of encouragement. I shook my head, and said, "I can only do what I can do," and let the gap between us widen. We both knew he was going to make the cutoff time, and we both knew that I might not. There really wasn't anything else to be said. A few minutes later he passed a woman wearing a bright pink running shirt, and then I lost sight of him altogether. But I was still running. I kept my eyes on the pink shirt, and step by step narrowed the gap.

Visibility was quite good on this stretch, with the road forming a long straightaway. Beyond that was a wall of green, a veritable rampart of steep, wooded hillside thrown across our path — the final climb that would take us high up above Multnomah Falls, then down the course's steepest descent on the far side before the flat stretch sweeping behind the lake and turning back to the finish line. The wall of green looked utterly impassable.

After a bit the course left the roadside and began winding through the woods again, starting with a gradual ascent that would become steeper and steeper. Although I didn't know it at the time, this stretch covered my second fastest mile of the day. I passed the lady in pink. We smiled at each other, each of us with breathing too shallow for words at this point. She passed me back a little later, and then slowed. In this way we leap frogged past each other, higher and higher, trying to show what encouragement we could. No one else was in sight, and the trail behind us for at least a good half mile was empty. In my judgment (mistaken as it turned out), we were the last two runners chasing the cutoff time. I didn't see how anyone further back would have a chance.

The trail turned to ascending switchbacks and steepened. The pink lady receded behind me. I ran any flat stretch, even if it was just 20 feet or so. I walked the rest, and mine was no longer a brisk walking pace. Higher and higher I trudged. Nausea slowly crept over me. Nothing felt appealing. Not water, which I continued to sip anyway, nor any of the food I had packed with me. My legs felt like rubber, and I leaned more heavily on my trekking poles. The grade steepened. The flat stretches shortened, and became less frequent.

I clambered up another sharp turn, and a longer flat stretch opened up in front of me. I willed my body once more to run, and I just couldn't. So I walked. I glanced at my watch, and realized 4 PM was coming up fast. By my estimation I was at least two miles from the next checkpoint, maybe further. At my current pace that was probably an hour or more away. And then what? Six rugged miles from there to the finish. At the end of the flat stretch was another climbing turn, and at the turn was a boulder about waist high. Looking up the hillside, I knew. The wax was melting from my wings, my feathers were falling, and this was as close to touching the sun as I dared reach on this day. Suddenly the boulder in front of me looked like the most comfortable chair I had ever seen, and with a deep sigh, I sat down.

For what seemed like a very long time, I just sat there. In actuality only a few minutes passed. The pink lady passed me, and I gave her a thumbs up. A couple of other runners shuffled by. I wasn't sure what to feel. Anger, frustration, and despair are all things I would have expected to feel as the reality of my first "Did Not Finish" began to sink in, but I felt none of those things. Mostly I was in a daze, only dimly aware of my surroundings.

Icarus flew alone, but I did not. Another runner approached, and he stopped.

"Are you okay?" he asked.

"I'm done," I replied flatly.

There was a long pause. Oddly, I found myself worrying about him. He was perilously close to missing the cutoff time at the final checkpoint, and I didn't want him missing it on my account. Finally he spoke. There are many things he could have said. He could have given the cheerful encouragement that runners so easily give each other, coaxing me to push on a little more. He did not.

Very matter of factly, he asked, "What are you going to do?"

I had been feeling detached, unable to focus. I still wasn't thinking clearly, but his words snapped my attention back into the present moment. Indeed, what was I going to do? I said simply, "I don't know."

"Well, you can go up or you can go down," he said, glancing at the parking lot hundreds of feet below us. He paused, and with just a hint of a smile, said "Down is easier than up. You may have a cell signal down there, or you may be able to catch a ride back to the finish area."

And just like that, the fog cleared from my thoughts. I said, "Yes, you're right. I'll go down. Thank you."

"No problem." He turned and headed up the trail.

"Good luck!" I called out.

He glanced back my way, genuinely smiling, and said, "Thanks."

I remained seated for another minute, gathering my strength and my thoughts for the walk down. And again I was not alone. She was a day hiker, and her name was Andrea. She asked me about the event, puzzled by the exhausted crowd sporting their numbered bibs that was passing her by. I explained about the race, and she asked me what I was doing. With a wry smile, I explained my predicament.

"Do you need a ride?"

"I would be incredibly grateful for a ride. And you would be my wife's hero for the day."

And so gingerly I made my way down to her car, and she drove me what seemed like a shockingly short distance back to Benson State Park and the finish area. We chatted. It turned out she was in the area on a spontaneous vacation. She lived and worked in New York City, but was growing tired of urban life. "It's just too far from real woods," she exclaimed at one point.

Some friends had connected her to some people in Portland who might be able to help her with a job search, and she had flown out to check out the area and get a sense of the Pacific Northwest lifestyle. That almost made me laugh out loud. You can't get more Pacific Northwest than an ultra run in the Columbia Gorge. Perhaps, in a wonderful bit of life's symmetries, I was in the right place at the right time for her as well.

When I walked up to Karen at the finish line she looked crestfallen. "I didn't see you come in," she said.

I, on the other hand, had never been so happy to see her. Regardless of the outcome, we now had the day as a shared experience, and that meant the world to me.

"I didn't finish," I told her. "But it's okay."

And it really was okay. I didn't understand why, but I didn't feel sad. Removing my bib, I sat down in a chair looking at the finish line. I had cold beer from a fresh tapped keg and food that suddenly looked delicious. There was live music from the band wafting in on the breeze, and all around me runners were celebrating. It was impossible not to feel happy.

Honestly that was the longest I have ever spent at the finish line of a race, and it was amazing. James, the race director, positioned himself at the finish line around noon, and for the next six hours he personally greeted and congratulated every single runner who came in. I saw runners come in laughing, and runners come in crying. Two guys actually sprinted the last 200 yards, and when they finished one turned to the other and said, "Thanks. I didn't think I was going to make it around the lake." Then they parted and went their separate ways, comrades, and maybe new found friends, who had only just met that day. Two women came in together, stride for stride, holding hands. Runners older and grayer than me crossed the finish line triumphantly.

I began to understand the source of my happiness. I was not alone. This was my community too.

About then I noticed that I had a text from Ken, time stamped 3:45.

He had texted when he reached the last checkpoint. "I made it with 40 to spare." At first this didn't make sense. Then it occurred to me that the organizers had decided to grant extra time because of the late start. That's what the woman at Checkpoint 2 had been calling out, I finally realized. What would I have done with an extra 20 minutes out there on the trail? Yet I sensed it didn't matter. I had traversed the narrow space between arrogance and humility and chosen correctly.

Based on Ken's pace up to Checkpoint 3, I figured he should reach the finish line around 5:15, and that's what I told Rose Mary. We could see the runners emerge from the far side of the lake, so the entire final quarter mile was in view. 5:15 came and went, and still no sign of Ken. Then 5:20. Then 5:25. Rose Mary was quiet, but I could see the anxiety written on her face.

Suddenly a thought occurred to me. For all Ken's long, diligent hours of incline training on the treadmill, there was one thing the treadmill did not prepare him for — downhill running. And the last leg included a merciless, steep, 1500 foot descent. Without thinking, without saying a word to anyone, I stood up and started walking the course backwards from the finish line, exactly the same path that Ken and I had traversed so very long ago that morning.

Runners passed me on their way to the finish, and I applauded and coaxed them on. None of them was Ken. I reached the lake, and began to see runners who had passed me on that last ascent. Still no sign of Ken. I left the lake behind, and walked towards Multnomah Falls. The pink lady approached, and I said, "You made it! Congratulations!" She beamed. Then I passed Multnomah Falls, and reached the base of the long, steep descent. I wasn't sure what burst of strength had carried me this far, but I knew I wasn't going to be able to climb much. Determined, I started up.

A few more runners passed me, and then the trail was empty. I looked at my watch; 5:42. Doubt crept in. Did I miss Ken? Was he already at the finish? Should I continue climbing up? Should I turn back? I started to turn back, and paused. Just one more minute, I told myself. Finally another runner rounded the hairpin turn above me, and sure enough — bright blue tech shirt, and bright green cap; it was Ken.

A smile burst onto his face as he walked up to me. "You made it!"

I smiled. "No, I dropped out. But you're going to make it. Come on. Let's go."

And suddenly we were running, together, and running felt like no effort at all. We chatted idly, and I have no recollection of what we said. I was just happy he was okay, and that we were together. The lake slipped by on our left, we rounded the final turn, and cruised towards the finish line. Daedalus and Icarus, together again. I dropped back, and let the cheers of the crowd and James's waiting congratulations carry Ken across the finish line. Then Rose Mary was in his arms, Karen embraced me, and I felt complete.

As my watch turned to 6:00 PM one more runner crossed the finish line. It was the guy who had stopped to talk with me. I went up to him and said, "Hey, you really saved my butt up there. That meant a lot to me when you had your own cutoff time to worry about."

"Well," he said, "it seemed important."

"Congrats on your finish. Well done."

Life guides us in ways we do not always understand. We end up in the right place at the right time, never having anticipated the moment, there for people we never knew we needed to be there for. We catch each other when we fall, so that when the sun rises each morning the Icarus within us can boldly rise again, reaching once more for new horizons. I can still vividly see, like a slow motion shot, Ken and I loping towards the finish line, James and Rose Mary eager to greet him, and me applauding him. And that very moment is just like the moment in my dream.

CHAPTER 22

MOTHER'S DAY

May 2013　|　Buckley, Washington

Dear Mother,

There's something I want you to understand about me and running. I know that the idea of me running marathon distances makes you anxious, and I want that to change. I want it to make you proud: not proud of me and what I've accomplished, but proud of yourself and what you've accomplished.

Friday evening Karen and I were watching Nathan swinging in the backyard, and remarking on how much his gross motor ability had improved, and how much more confident he was as a result. In particular, he had gotten really good at getting the swing up high and then jumping off. Karen said, "It's good to see him so bold… as long as he stays within my comfort zone."

That's really one of the great paradoxes of parenting, and motherhood in particular, isn't it? You want your children to approach life boldly and yet somehow stay within your own comfort zone when it comes to their safety and well being.

Obviously I grew up in a very intellectual setting — both you and Daddy and now both your children have at least a master's degree and a lifelong engagement with learning. But what I appreciate so much about my upbringing was how I was encouraged to develop a life of the body, not just a life of the mind, and to see these two as in harmony.

I don't want to diminish Daddy's contribution in this regard. I think of all the time he spent with me playing tennis, basketball, throwing a frisbee, and just playing catch. And I think of how he showed me the mental side of sports, whether it was watching the Cardinals play baseball or watching John Newcombe on the tennis court. But to some extent that's what's expected in father-son relationships. So I appreciate what he gave me, but I also expected it.

What's more remarkable is the role that you played. You are the one who pushed me to get involved with Boys' Club, and to sign up for their basketball team. You are the one who carpooled me to all of those games, including neighborhoods in D.C. that nice suburban white boys weren't supposed to go to (not that I knew that at the time; you and Daddy raised me to be blind to those distinctions). And while I know that you and Daddy both watched my games at the end of University of Maryland basketball camp, my most vivid memory is of you, just beaming with pride, at the defensive job I put on my matchup in the finals of the 3-on-3 tournament. I've never told you straight out how much your pride in me meant, but I want to say that now.

And you had your own sports heroes that inspired me, and from whom I learned through you. I learned to play hard, but fair, and always to play smart. The Billie Jean King — Bobby Riggs match was a formative experience for me, not so much from watching her as from watching you watching her. Your pride and your sense of mission in that moment told me that the only barriers to what is possible are the barriers we impose on ourselves.

Not long after that I began to leave behind the sports with which you were familiar, and to move beyond your comfort zone. In retrospect, when I realize how little about rock climbing you knew, and thus how little you knew about how safe it could be, I'm astonished you let me pursue that endeavor. But you did, and never once criticized or openly fretted over my choice. That must have been hard.

Of course you might also consider how much your own enthusiasm for the story of Tenzing Norgay climbing Everest inspired my interest in things like rock climbing and backpacking. As I think back, though, I realize that many stories that you loved were stories of people discovering through their engagement with Nature a way to break free from the limits society had defined for them. Think of Katherine Hepburn's character in one of your favorite movies, The African Queen. Or your admiration for Karen Blixen and one of your favorite books, Out of Africa. Of course, for you it was important that many of these heroes were women, and the societal limits they were transcending were gender-based. For me they were simply people striving to discover and become themselves. But I am acutely aware that I owe that insight to you, and to the passion for these stories that you shared with me.

Now, decades and two back surgeries later, at age 53, here I am running. And not just running, but pushing marathon distances.

But here's the thing. Friday night before bed I was doing my preparation for my long Saturday run. My training plan called for a 20-mile run, and since my next race is at elevation I do those training runs up in Mount Rainier National Park. It involves running ten miles up a 4% grade, which any runner will tell you is a monstrous amount of elevation gain for a single run. I have to carry enough water, and some sort of carbohydrate and electrolyte supplement. I need to think about the variable weather conditions, since I start at about 1500 feet elevation but will reach my turnaround point near the snow pack. I need to be self-aware and disciplined enough to know what pace I can manage that will build my body up rather than tear it down, and leave me enough recoverable stamina for the remainder of the week's workouts. There is an enormous amount of thought and planning that goes into this, and it is all part of a larger and more complex thought process about how to run a marathon, a distance that the human body is not naturally able to sustain, but that no other animal on the planet handles so ably. It isn't just a physical test, it is a test of will and a test of intellect.

And as I'm going through my ritual of preparations, in the background I can hear a TV interview with Jimmy Conners, now 60 years old with a just published autobiography. I hear him talking about his training routine when he was on the pro tour, and his mental preparation before a match. Of course he talks about his US Open victory, in five sets, at age 39, over a young and in his prime Aaron Krickstein. I remember that match, and was riveted watching it on TV. Suddenly I'm struck by a sense of common spirit. I'm no Jimmy Conners; of course I know that. But the meditative preparation, the ritualistic fussing with gear, the thought and preparation before a daunting task. These are things all runners, and indeed all athletes, have in common.

That's when I realize I'll probably never win a race. I will set no records of note. No sports story will ever mention my name. But I am not the old man with the broken back and the half dead right foot. I am an athlete. And you made it possible for me to be that way. Because you, more than any other single person in my life, taught me to live without barriers and without limitations.

So I want to thank you for that. And I want you to be proud. I want you to be proud of your achievement in laying this foundation in me. Please remember that deep inside I am still just your little boy trying to figure out how to be a man.

Happy Mother's Day,

Your son Mark

CHAPTER 23

BECAUSE THAT'S WHERE THE CAR IS

September 2015 | Mount Rainier National Park

When I resumed running in 2009 I didn't have any organized plan other than to get back in shape and return to a pastime that I loved. My first day out I covered a mile and a half at a slow jog, and I had to stop twice to catch my breath. I don't even remember what prompted me to sign up for the Seattle 15K in spring of 2011, but I guess I felt that after two years of steadily improved running, I needed to mark my progress in some way.

The race itself, a beautiful course circumnavigating Lake Union in Seattle with an out and back leg in the direction of the Ballard Locks, was farther than I had ever run.

The race was an energizing, uplifting experience. I needed another goal, so I signed up for the Black Diamond Half Marathon in fall of 2011. My longest training run prior was 12 miles, and that was farther than I had ever run.

The race itself, starting and ending at Nolte State Park and looping through the farmland between the towns of Enumclaw and Black Diamond, was farther than I had ever run.

My time was a little over two hours, not bad for a 51 year old running his first half marathon. But I went out too fast, bonked pretty hard at the end, and knew I could do better. I spent the next six months working on shorter distances and improving my speed. Then I worked on maintaining that speed as I built stamina, aiming towards the Capital City Half Marathon in Olympia in May of 2012. Somewhere in April I cranked out a 15 mile training run, and again that was farther than I had ever run.

My Capital City time was very satisfying, coming in at 1:56:20. Daunting as it seemed, the obvious next challenge was a full marathon, and so I signed up for the Seattle Marathon, scheduled for November 2012. Tough as that race was, it opened up a world of running to me, and gave me a chance to say, "Today I have run farther than I have ever run before."

Even then, in the back of my mind, a little voice that grew louder with time, asked, "Will I ever run farther?"

For a while I had no shortage of running goals. I wanted to set a new PR at the half marathon. It took me a couple of tries, but in October of 2013 at the Run Like Hell Half Marathon in Portland, I did. I wanted to run a full marathon where I didn't bonk, where I could finish without feeling like I had utterly suffered. It took me a couple of tries, but in May of 2014 at the Capital City Marathon in Olympia, I did.

The finish line in Olympia was a great moment, with my Nathan and Karen right there. But it was also the first time in quite a while when I felt like I didn't have a next running goal. At 54, I didn't see myself getting a lot faster. And the older I got, the more I found road racing really beat up my body. And thanks to time spent on Mount Rainier, I had fallen in love with trail running. The solitude and sanctuary of nature that I loved from camping and backpacking came together with the deep, meditative state that I cherish on long, slow runs. Days running up on Mount Rainier were perfect days. So after Capital City I knew my next race had to be a trail race.

If we don't fail at times in life then we aren't really trying hard enough. We aren't facing big enough challenges, we aren't taking enough risks. My DNF at Gorge Waterfalls 50K taught me that I had a lot to learn about ultra running, and a lot to learn about adapting to trail running. That spring and summer I pondered what I needed to change. Was running five days a week in training instead of my usual four just too hard on my body? Or did I not run enough training miles? Were training runs with 3000 feet of elevation gain enough? Or should I have done more hill work? Did I let the difficulty of the course intimidate me? (Perhaps.) Was it a mistake to eat or drink nothing through the first nine miles of the race? (Yes.) Beyond marathon distances we are pushing the human body to the limits of what is possible, and so it does not take a big error for an entire race to unravel.

And so I found myself without a clear running goal. I knew I wanted to do a fall race, and I wanted to get more familiar with trail racing. Defiance 50K, scheduled for October 10, caught my eye. In addition to the 50K they also ran a 30K and 15K at the same time, and I found myself thinking that the 30K sounded like a good way to get in a decent trail race and work my way back towards another 50K attempt.

To be clear, I didn't really have a training plan. With my three marathons and most of my half marathons I'd been very precise, working out a detailed week by week plan. For my 50K attempt in March I did the same thing. While I think it helped to have that discipline training through dark, wet, cold, winter months, I think I also felt a fair amount of training burnout by the time I got to the end of it. So, for most of this year I really just focused on running for fun.

One of the best running decisions I've made was to finally buy an annual pass to the National Park system. I can be in Mount Rainier National Park in 40 minutes from my driveway, and the trails up there are spectacular. Where I run there are two main trailheads. One is all the way up at Mowich Lake, around 5000 feet in elevation. From here one can follow the Wonderland Trail down the steep descent along Mowich River, or follow Wonderland in the opposite direction through Ipsut Pass and down the deep valley carved out by Ipsut Creek. Alternatively one can fork off the Wonderland Trail up to Spray Park, crossing 6000 feet in elevation, with the snow cap of Mount Rainier so close you feel like you could just reach out and touch it.

The other trailhead is just past the Carbon River entrance to the park. You follow the Carbon River for five miles until you intersect with the Wonderland Trail at Ipsut Creek after it has tumbled down from Ipsut Pass. From here you have several choices for destinations: the steep climb up to Green Lake, the more gradual climb up to Carbon Glacier, the side trail off the Carbon Glacier trail that takes you up and over the ridgeline to Windy Gap, or the intimidating ascent up Cataract Valley. This last trail takes you through the woods on endless switchbacks, across shale and loose rock as you leave the tree line, and finally into the snow line itself, well above 6000 feet.

Over the course of the spring and summer I ran many of these routes, running without regard for distance or pace, mainly just enjoying the scenery, immersing myself in nature, and just making sure I spent reasonable time on feet for my runs.

All this time I had it in my head that I was signing up for a 30K trail run in October. As August approached I increased the intensity of my runs, putting a bit more distance and elevation gain into my weekend long runs. Early in August I completed a 15-mile run along the Carbon River with about 2000 feet of elevation gain. I realized that with a training run like that I felt completely ready for a 30K on flatter terrain. And I realized I was early. The race was still more than two months away.

On a whim, I pushed my training further. Long runs extended to more like 20 miles, often with five to six hours of time on feet, and elevation gain that was a minimum of 2500 feet. Yes, I was going for it. I was going to sign up for the 50K, and take another shot at the distance that had eluded me in March.

Trail runners inevitably miscalculate. We make a mistake in planning, and sometimes we compound that with tunnel vision on the trail that leads to poor decisions, on rare occasions putting ourselves in jeopardy. I've been guilty of that a few times, and each time I tell myself "never again."

On September 5 I left the house pre-dawn, driving up to Mowich Lake. My intent was to run a classic route followed by local ultra runners called simply "The Loop". From Mowich Lake it climbs to Ipsut Pass, then drops all the way to the confluence of Ipsut Creek and Carbon River. The route then follows the river to just below Carbon Glacier before veering off to wind up Cataract Valley emerging at Spray Park. It then descends back down to Mowich Lake. All told about 20 miles of the most gorgeous scenery anywhere in Mount Rainier National Park.

Since parts of this route were unfamiliar to me, I had picked up a trail map from the Park Service. Glancing at it before leaving the house, I read Ipsut Creek Campground as 4200 feet elevation, and Spray Park as 4800 feet. So I assumed once I made the descent from Ipsut Pass I was looking at 600 feet of elevation gain. There were several problems with this assumption. First, I had transposed the numbers when reading Ipsut Creek Campground; it's actually at 2400 feet. Second, the 4800 feet referred to Cataract Valley Campground, which is only part way up Cataract Valley. The ridgeline summit of that section of trail is well above 6000 feet. So of course I only took clothing with me appropriate for a September run below the snow line: a long sleeve tech shirt and a light windbreaker.

The day started well. I'd run the stretch up to Ipsut Pass many times, and I was eager to cross the Pass for the first time. I relished the steep descent on the other side, with its soaring, cathedral-like views of the surrounding cliffs. The flatter stretch along Carbon River was also familiar to me, and I'm always in awe of the sudden view of the summit of Mount Rainier after crossing the Carbon River. By the time I reached the suspension bridge below Carbon Glacier I felt the exertion, but I felt in control.

The next three hours were a battle. I'd never been in Cataract Valley before, but it quickly became apparent that I'd wildly miscalculated the elevation gain on today's course. This stretch alone was over 3000 feet of climb, and it was unrelenting; never a step of level ground, never a step of downhill. The average grade along this section is greater than 10%. The mountain played head games with me, each ridgeline looking like it would be the summit, only to reveal itself as a shoulder hiding the next ridgeline beyond it. Somehow I kept going.

In the back of my mind it began to dawn on me that as the day wore on the temperature was actually dropping. I had long ago removed the windbreaker, soaked with sweat, and stashed it in my pack. As I left the treeline and moved into the clouds during my ascent I realized that the steady mountain breeze cutting through my damp shirt was chilling me.

I couldn't continue to divide my energy reserve between core warmth and exertion for the climb. I had to find a way to avoid crossing the line into even mild hypothermia.

I stopped and pulled my windbreaker out of my pack. It was still soaked. Feeling the breeze, I played a hunch that it would dry quickly. I strapped it to the outside of my pack and kept running. About 15 minutes later I stopped again, and sure enough my windbreaker was dry. There was now snow on the ground all around me. Quickly I put on my windbreaker, and moved on. It worked. With a dry shell between me and the wind I felt the chill receding, and I felt more energy to push through the climb.

When I finally reached the summit ridge above Spray Park I was completely spent. Wobbly legs, light headed, queasy stomach; I had hit "the Wall" and then some. Looking at the map, I could see that I had seven miles to go. Even though it was mostly downhill at this point, I had no idea where I would find the strength to cover seven miles. All I could do was tell myself, "No one is coming up here to help you down. So suck it up, buttercup; you have to finish. Because that's where the car is."

I came out of the snow. I came out of the clouds. I mustered a crooked smile for the cheery day hikers making their way up from the other side. I caught the gleam of Mowich Lake through the trees. At last I found the car.

And for the rest of my training, and all through the looming battle that would be the Defiance 50K, I never forgot that day. I had faced the mountain, and endured. If I could finish that run, I could do anything.

CHAPTER 24

BACKPACKER BORN

September 2015 | Mount Rainier National Park

Every summer Nathan and I take at least one camping trip. This summer slipped away from me, as my weekends were focused on getting in my long runs in preparation for the Defiance 50K. Now, though, I'm in my tapering down period right before the race, and this particular weekend is set aside for camping.

Friday morning I drive up to the Carbon River Ranger Station to see about a camping permit. I'm hoping for Ipsut Creek, which has dozens of tent sites, but they are full up for the weekend. Instead it will be Eagle's Roost, a shorter but steeper hike in. At least the trail will be familiar to Nathan from our training runs last year.

Friday evening we lay out all our gear. I've purchased a small backpack for him, and he'll be carrying his clothes and his sleeping bag. The tent, sleeping pads, my sleeping bag and all of our food will be in my pack.

That pack has seen some miles. I've had it since before Nathan was born, and indeed since before his older brother Alex was born. It has taken me along countless miles of the Pacific Crest Trail in California, especially around the headwaters of the Feather River. It has taken me to Alaska, and along the Chilcoot Trail, over the Golden Staircase, to the headwaters of the Yukon River. This weekend will be a less ambitious trip than those, but no less significant. The first father-son backpacking trip is a parenting milestone.

We drive a little over an hour from the house up to Mowich Lake. The last 15 miles of dirt and gravel now has the comforting familiarity of an old friend, representing hundreds of training miles I have run over the last several years. The morning is still early, but already the parking lot is filling up. Shouldering our packs, we set off through the trees.

Every time I take Nathan into the wilderness I marvel at the change that comes over him. He fidgets and fusses and chatters away constantly, much as he does at home. "What kind of bird is that?" "My belt's too tight." "Do you think we'll see any bears?" "My shoulders hurt; this strap is rubbing." Then, as the quiet of the mountains settles over him, his mind relaxes, and slows down. The conversation carries on, but tempered with long stretches of silence, where we just look and listen to our surroundings.

Our trail joins the Wonderland Trail, and we complete the first long climb up the ridge, under the canopy of pines, crossing over the spur of the ridge to the other side. The slope is steeper here as our trail snakes along. Then we emerge from the trees to an open space formed by a massive rock slide years ago. We pick our way across the scree, and Nathan looks around appraisingly.

"It looks like cobblestone," he says, and continues, "What kind of biome do you think this is?"

He's referencing Minecraft, the computer game that has become another big bonding opportunity for us. I reply, "Forest biome for sure."

He nods, and says, "We should have brought a pickaxe. And an axe. We could make a house!"

"Well, crafting in real life is a little harder than Minecraft. And I don't think the rangers would appreciate it. Besides, the game mode here is peaceful; I don't think we need to worry about hostile mobs."

He laughs, and we continue. Another steep climb and a short hike over a flat stretch along the ridgetop, and we come to Eagle Cliff. Here we pause for lunch and take in the view. Spray Creek sparkles far below, and across the valley we have a panoramic view of Russell Glacier, feeding snowmelt into the river. Towering above all is the mighty snowcap of Mount Rainier, rising to Liberty Cap.

We linger for a while, soaking it all in. At last we shoulder our packs and complete the last easy mile to where Eagle's Roost campground is nestled among the trees. No campfires are permitted here, but I have my little cooking stove, and a Coleman lantern, making it cozy enough.

In the morning we leave our packs behind for a day hike. Less than a mile from the campground we come to Spray Falls. Here the creek tumbles down a thousand feet from the ridgeline above, the last fifty feet or so rushing over a cliff in a spectacular waterfall. We spend a few minutes taking in the view, and then begin our ascent.

The trail here is all switchbacks, and even so the average grade is about 10%. Nathan grumbles, and we take many rest breaks, but he is resolute about completing the climb.

At last we complete the switchbacks. The trail is still climbing here, but at a much gentler incline. A few minutes of hiking brings us out of the trees into a small meadow. We duck in and out of woods a few more times, but over the next half hour the space around us opens up more and more. Then we emerge onto a broad, alpine meadow — Spray Park. To our left the meadow rises to a high ridgeline, where even the grass, wildflowers, and scrub brush peter out, leaving nothing but rock and Rainier's distinctive powdery volcanic ash. Here the ridgeline tops 6000 feet before descending to Seattle Park on the other side. Ahead and to our right, across the meadow, Rainier's snowcap greets us, rising first to Liberty Cap, and then all the way to the summit. It feels as close — and as far — as a mirage.

Nathan and I spend a long while in Spray Park, mostly in silence. Occasionally other hikers pass by, some for whom this is their destination, others weighed down with heavy packs continuing along the Wonderland Trail. Nathan's posture is relaxed, tranquil, but his eyes are wide. He looks reverent. I'm sure I do too. This is the part of Mount Rainier that has to be experienced to be truly understood.

At last I nudge him. "Come on," I say. "We should head back down. Mom will be worried about us if we get home too late."

And so we cross the meadow, descend the switchbacks, pack up our camp, and shouldering our packs, make our way back towards Mowich Lake. Nathan grumbles a bit about the weight of his pack and the distance to the car. But as we traverse up the last ridge before turning down to the lake, Nathan turns, looks back over his shoulder at me and says, "This is the best day ever."

I grin, and think to myself, "Right back at you, buddy."

CHAPTER 25

HURRICANE OHO

October 2015　|　Tacoma, Washington

The rain eases slightly, and I glance at my GPS watch: 26.7 miles. "Today I have run farther than I have ever run before." As runners, how many times do we get to say that?

Any ultra is a leap of faith, but this certainly was not the race I had expected. October is usually a fabulous weather month in the Pacific Northwest. Temperatures have moderated, but the rainy season has yet to start. For runners this time of year promises blue skies and temperatures in the 50s to 60s, pretty much ideal running conditions. 2015, however, was shaping up to be an El Nino year, meaning a longer and wetter rainy season, as well as more variance in conditions.

As October 10 approached the forecast appeared to settle in on cloudy, cool, with scattered rain showers. That didn't phase me; I ran my first five races in the Pacific Northwest in at least partial rain.

Predominant high pressure systems over the North Pacific keep tropical storms at bay. Systems that form around Hawaii tend to blow towards the south and west. Occasionally Hawaii experiences something called Kona Winds, in which the prevailing wind direction reverses, sending storms to the Northwest. Generally these tropical depressions lose force as they move north, but on very rare occasions they gain storm strength after leaving the tropics. Scientists have had to coin the term "extra-tropical storm" for these, since technically they can't be called tropical storms. Prior to 2015, the last time one of these made landfall in the Pacific Northwest was 1949.

So with less than a week to go until race day, I was a little alarmed to read news reports about something headed in our direction called Hurricane Oho. Centered around Ketchikan, Alaska when it finally made landfall the night of October 9, the storm would have wide ranging effects along the Alaskan coast, throughout British Columbia, and down into Washington and Oregon.

Point Defiance, where our race course was laid out, is a narrow, rugged spit of land that juts out into the water, dividing Puget Sound from Commencement Bay. Even in the best of times this stretch is notorious for high winds. Our forecast for race day was steady rain, winds averaging 15 MPH with gusts up to 50 MPH. Karen wondered if it might be prudent to take a pass on this race. But having taken a DNF in my previous 50K attempt I was determined to see this through, and no runner likes to waste months of training.

Tacoma, Washington is not an obvious locale for a 50K trail run. Washington's third largest city is a densely populated, mainly blue collar city wedged between Joint Base Lewis-McChord to the east and the Puget Sound to the west. It straddles the hilly peninsula that splits Commencement Bay to the north from the main body of the Sound that passes to the west and south of the city.

At the very tip of this peninsula lies Point Defiance Park, 702 acres of old growth forest on the bluffs above Owen Beach and the rest of the waterfront. The forest has trees as much as 500 years old. Single track dirt trails criss-cross throughout the park, feeling like high arched tunnels through the surrounding greenery. The trails occasionally burst out of the trees to an overlook offering spectacular views of the sweeping majesty of the Tacoma Narrows Bridge, or the Vashon Island Ferry quietly plying the water between Point Defiance and Tahlequah. No section of the course is flat, but there are no long, sustained climbs either.

And Defiance 50K would not be what it is without Nelly's Gnarly Descent, a quarter mile rough cut trail descending sharply from the bluffs to Owen Beach, and requiring three fixed place rappel lines to safely navigate the descent.

The race starts at Owen Beach, heading east along the boardwalk, before climbing a staircase to the bluff above and beginning the winding criss-cross of dirt trails through the forest, emerging at Fort Nisqually, and then diving back into the forest before finally emerging from the base of Nelly's Gnarly Descent for a short 100 yard dash to the finish line at Owen Beach. There's a 15K that completes one loop of this course, a 30K that completes two loops, and the 50K that completes three loops.

There's an aid station at the start / finish area at Owen Beach, and another aid station at Fort Nisqually around Mile 5. It's net uphill, with lots of ups and downs to Fort Nisqually, and an equally uneven net downhill back to Owen Beach.

A 45 minute drive takes me from my house to Point Defiance Park, and when I depart at 6:30 AM gusting winds drive an angry mix of black storm clouds around the sky, broken up by streaks of blue sky. There is no rain. The temperature is 70F, about 20 degrees above the norm for October at that hour of the morning. I've been watching the Hurricane Oho reports closely all week, but as I near Point Defiance Park the blue sky increases. I'm starting to wonder if the storm already passed through overnight.

I park at the Boat Launch. It's a half mile from the starting line, but the course goes right by here, which enables me to use my car as a personal aid station. I lay out my fuel pack, my watch, my trail mix, and in a last minute decision pull off my windbreaker and long sleeve shirt in exchange for just a short sleeve shirt. I make the walk to the starting line, get checked in, and get my bib pinned on. By the time I'm done with all this we have only about five minutes until start.

I'm surprisingly calm. I don't have a real race plan other than don't start too fast, and while I feel confident in my training I know it's been pretty informal by my standards. Still, I'm relaxed and ready at the start. The 15K, 30K, and 50K all start together, and so we have hundreds of runners gathered at the start, even though less than 100 of us are here for the 50K. After months of training in solitude, I enjoy the quiet camaraderie of all these runners gathered and ready to begin an endeavor together.

The horn sounds, and we start. I focus on staying in the back of the pack, thinking over and over in my head, "Don't start too fast." Nonetheless, the first two miles go by quickly.

Then the rain starts. At first, it's just a drizzle, more heard than felt as the gentle patter quietly cascades through the canopy above. As we approach Mile 4, the sky opens into a downpour. I'm soaked, but I feel elated. It's warm, and the air smells fresh, and I'm surrounded by enthusiastic runners. We are Pacific Northwest runners. This is what we train for. This is what we train in. Realizing that my shirt is only weighing me down at this point, I duck into a covered picnic area, strip off and wring out my shirt, and stuff it in my fuel pack. I run the rest of the first loop topless. There will be a price paid for this in chafed skin from my fuel pack straps, but that's a future problem. In the moment I don't care.

About a mile from Fort Nisqually we reach a steep uphill that runs some 300 yards. The downpour has unleashed a mini flash flood coursing down the trail here, and our pack of runners has no choice but to plunge in and slog our way up. About halfway up I hear a panicked cry of "I'm not going to make it!" from the woman behind me. Glancing over my shoulder, I see her standing there paralyzed. She's wearing a large brace on her right knee. She looks up at me and says, "My knee. I don't think I can do this." I reach down, clasping her arm, and try to say with as much calm as I can muster, "Come on. We're all in this together." Between the mud, and the torrent of streaming water, my own purchase is far from secure. Hand in hand, step by step, she and I make our way to the top of this stretch until the terrain flattens, and water ebbs, and it's possible to run again. She flashes me a thankful smile, I give her a thumbs up, and take off up the trail.

Fort Nisqually is a gorgeously restored 19th century wooden palisade fort, a classic example of the trapping and trading outpost so common to the early European settlers in this region. On the other side of the grassy field behind the fort is the small pavilion tent that marks the aid station. Taking another lesson from past races, I am drinking water and snacking on my trail mix early and often. I opt not to stop at the aid station, and plunge into the forest once again. The next section presents a lot of short, steep hills with a winding trail, and dirt that has not quite turned to mud. After a couple of miles the trail widens, but also frequently fills with puddles. There's no longer any point in dodging them, and this stretch is mostly downhill, so I just charge straight ahead through the rain and the puddles on the most direct path I can find.

By the time I reach Nelly's Gnarly Descent, the rain has tapered back down to a drizzle. I stumble through the first couple of switchbacks due to the mud, and at one point the only way I can brake my descent is to crash into and hug a tree trunk. Then I reach the rappel lines. I navigate the first two successfully, and I'm feeling pretty proud of myself. Then right at the base of the third line my feet go out from under me, and down I go. As I reach Owen Beach and the finish area both hands are covered in mud and I have a long muddy streak that extends all the way from my hip to my left ankle. Fortunately there's a sink at the finish area, and I wash up as best I can. I glance at the clock, and the happy 15K runners who are crossing the line and done for the day. 1 hour 45 minutes. Much faster than I need to be to stay ahead of the 8 hour cut off time. Quickly I move out to start the second loop, and more importantly get to my car half a mile away.

I spend 20 minutes at the car. Huddled under the raised hatch in the back to stay somewhat dry, I do a complete change of clothes, except for my wet shoes, putting on something dry from head to toe. I swap in a fresh pack of trail mix, check the water level in my fuel pack, and set off.

The rain has mostly stopped. Patches of blue sky are visible. It remains this way for most of Loop 2. This time around, everything feels quiet. Instead of being surrounded by a crowd of eager 15K runners, I am running in solitude. I spot an occasional 30K or 50K runner through the trees, but mostly I am nestled deep in the serenity of quiet trails through old growth forest. Now that the ground has absorbed the rain, the mud is much worse. The hilly switchbacks after Fort Nisqually have become treacherous; to keep my footing I have to take the downhills even slower than the uphills. I mud ski down the last of these, and the course opens up once again to wider, flatter trails.

A few minutes later, around Mile 18, I spot another runner up ahead, steadily walking along. I'm feeling fatigued, but not spent, trying not to think about the fact that I still have a half marathon to go. I pull up next to her, and slow to a walk. Her name is Kathleen, and she is also signed up for the 50K. I ask her how she's doing.

She smiles grimly and says, "I think I'm dropping out at Mile 20. Today just isn't my day." She pauses, and continues, "I've had a pretty aggressive summer of racing, and my knee has been acting up. The mud has been really hard on it today, and I don't want to push too much. This is just a training run anyway."

A note to all you non-runners: that last statement is a lie. Yes, we runners often work a scheduled race into our training plans where the training goal is a different race later on. But come game day, we are all the same. We all want to compete, we all want to give our best effort. There are no "training runs" on game day.

Kathleen and I walk and chat for a few minutes, swapping stories about races and courses in the area. I listen with interest as she talks about trail running on Mount Hood, and she expresses genuine interest in the Winthrop Marathon and the North Cascades area generally. I wish her well, urge her to be careful, resume running, and move on. I feel some reluctance; it has been lonely out here on Loop 2, and just having Kathleen to talk to has lifted my spirits. Perhaps I have done the same for her. I won't know for several days yet when results are posted, but Kathleen will in fact finish. A mere seven minutes ahead of the cutoff time, but a finish nonetheless. As I said, game day.

This time I navigate Nelly's Gnarly Descent more gracefully, making it to the bottom without a fall. The rain is starting to pick up again. I wave to the volunteers as I pass the finish area and begin Loop 3, the final loop. It has taken me 2 hours 45 minutes to complete the second loop, almost an hour longer than the first. With the 20 minute car break and the walking time with Kathleen that isn't too surprising. I am moving more slowly overall, but I'm still well ahead of cutoff pace. Back at my car I take a shorter break this time. I spend about ten minutes changing into dry clothing from the waist up and then I'm on the move again.

I'm tired. But I also know that I have banked enough time to complete the final loop at a moderately brisk walk, if need be. It's the last loop, and as far as I know I am DFL ("dead f'ing last" in running vernacular). In the next mile or so I catch up to two women running together. They look relaxed, keeping a comfortable pace and quietly chatting. They step aside for me as I get close to them, and I smile and nod and move on. On the longer straight stretches I can see two men up ahead of me, and they appear to be switching back and forth, jockeying for position. We're still on the uphill portion leading to Fort Nisqually, and so I'm wary of pushing too hard to try and close with them.

Abruptly the sky darkens, the temperature drops noticeably, and the sighing wind explodes into a howl. The sky opens, and the rain comes down in torrents. The rain is literally blowing sideways, and I can barely see more than a few feet in front of me. The wind is so loud I can't hear myself think. The wrath of the wind takes its toll on the forest. I am pelted by pine cones knocked loose; I see branches down on the trail; I hear the crashing of tree limbs newly torn free by the storm. I am completely soaked through, and the temperature is no longer warm enough for me to shrug it off. The force of it all has left me shell shocked. For the next couple of miles the storm has me beaten down to a basic animal level where all I can do is shuffle forward one step at a time, sometimes running, but just as often walking.

Eventually the thinning of the trees tells me I'm approaching Fort Nisqually. Dimly I wonder if they might call the race for safety reasons. Part of me wonders if I'd be grateful, but the louder voice in my head fiercely says, "No!" I will finish this course, on my own if I have to."

The wooden palisade wall of the fort provides brief respite from the wind. Indeed, as I reach the field beyond the wind has died down, though the downpour continues unrelenting. I reach the aid station, and this last time through I am ready to take a break. I spend a few minutes chatting with the women who are volunteering, and giving them a truly heartfelt thanks. These are horrendous conditions to be outside, and they have only their small tent canopy for cover. At least I can keep moving to stay warm.

One thing I've learned over the years is that, at this stage of a race, I should abandon any preconceived notions of what I'll rely on for fuel and simply listen to my body. The urges that sweep over me are always amusing and surprising. Today is no exception. "Mountain Dew? This stuff is amazing! Pretzels? Perfect! How many can I take?" I also discover that my fuel pack is now empty, and the volunteers help me refill it.

As I'm pulling out of the aid station I see the two women behind me rounding the corner of Fort Nisqually and heading across the field. A little over 25 miles done. A little over five miles to go. One last time I descend into the hilly switchbacks and the mudfest that awaits. I get occasional glimpses of one of the men ahead of me as he steps gingerly through the mud.

Somewhere in the next few miles it dawns on me that I haven't really hit "the Wall." Yes, I'm fatigued. No, I don't have a lot left. But I feel nothing like the crushing psychological darkness that descended on me in my first two marathons. I've experienced nothing like the rubber-legged, light headed wooziness with which I stumbled through my last couple of miles at Gorge Waterfalls 50K, muscles literally feeling like they were on fire. The confidence I've nurtured all day is swelling up inside me around a rock hard, solid core of determination. I'm going to make it. I'm going to finish. I am an ultra runner. Then I look down at my watch.

26.7 miles. "Today I have run farther than I have ever run before." Suddenly I am weeping. All the emotions have bubbled over, and I am standing in the middle of the trail sobbing openly. This is the part of distance running, the spiritual challenge, that is so hard to explain to non-runners. 27 miles in, and you have no energy for anything, except to be utterly and completely who you are, stripped down to the most naked essence of your soul.

And then I am running. I don't even know how. Not walking, not shuffling along, not jogging, but flat out running, faster than I have run all day. And it feels effortless. The trail has widened, turned mostly downhill, and I am bounding down, through the rain, through the puddles, with a lightness that is normally reserved for my dreams.

I catch the guy in front of me just as we reach a road crossing, and we are greeted with the bizarre sight of a traffic jam. He glances at the front of the line of cars and says, "Tree down." I follow his stare, and sure enough a massive tree has fallen across the road. I think of everything Hurricane Oho has thrown at me on this day — the lashing rain, the howling wind, the downed branches, the mud. I think to myself, "Oho, you have challenged me, but nothing has tested me like Mount Rainier." I think back to that day, only a month ago, standing above Spray Park in the snow, cold and spent from the grueling ascent up Cataract Valley. I feel for where I had to dig down inside myself, and realize that day made me ready for this day, for I do not have to dig that deep. I look now at the storm around me and feel capable and defiant. Crossing the road, I take off at a dash, leaving the other runner behind me.

The euphoria subsides, but never completely goes away. My pace eases, but I'm still running hard. I relish the rain on my face. I eagerly seek out every puddle. About a half mile down the trail I catch the other guy. As I flash past him, I call out, "Hell of a day for a run!" I'm sure the grin on my face is ear to ear. He just looks at me like I'm crazy. At this moment, I probably am. When I emerge from the trees to the top of Nelly's Gnarly Descent I'm almost sad. As with reading a cherished book, part of me doesn't want this race to end.

I make my way, one last time down the rappel lines, and for the first time since the Fort Nisqually aid station I am conscious of just how fatigued I really am. I simply haven't the strength to stay on my feet through this descent. The last 20 feet is just a slide on my butt. Then it's done. Muddy, bloody, and sweaty, I stand with 100 yards of waterfront boardwalk between me and the finish line. Pride conquers fatigue, and I run. I hear people cheering in the rain, and the finish line volunteer calling out my name, and I am grateful for the rain for a whole different reason. The tears are back, but on my rain-streaked face as I cross the finish line no one seems to notice.

7 hours, 27 minutes, 57 seconds. 31 miles, run and done. I may never get to say it again, but I can say it now — today I have run farther than I have ever run before.

Chamber
of
GO
WHITE
RIVER

CHAPTER 26

TRACK MEET

May 2016 | Buckley, Washington

Jaw set, eyes staring at the white marker before the sand pit, Nathan is a model of focus and determination, oblivious to the rain dripping off of his nose and the fact that his clothes are completely soaked. A quick intake of breath, and then he is off at a sprint. The resulting long jump will put him in the middle of the standings, but he looks proud, and rightly so.

In a few minutes the 50-meter dash will commence, and when he crosses the finish line in the final of the three heats, he will take third place. A very respectable outcome for an 11 year old who is, at heart, an ordinary runner. Of course the deepest lesson I have taken from the running community is that every ordinary run happens at the end of a unique journey for that runner that is, in its own way, extraordinary. Nathan is no exception.

And neither am I.

At this point Nathan has completed not just the Run for Jacoby 5K, but the Run Wild 5K at Northwest Trek. Northwest Trek Wildlife Park is oriented around creatures native to the Pacific Northwest housed in something close to their natural habitat, and the annual run through the park is a unique experience. We did this event as a family, with Karen doing the 5k walk while Nathan and I did the run together.

We also did the event in the pouring rain, which is often just a fact of life in the Pacific Northwest. Nathan has grown into a true native of the area — eager to spend time outdoors, and undaunted by the weather.

After Nathan's two 5Ks, Karen and I signed him up to do track and field in 4th grade, and again in 5th. At the elementary school level track and field consists of two months of practice culminating in a single district wide track meet.

Nathan's first track meet was a disaster. I made the critical parenting mistake of letting my ambitions for him get in the way of what best suited him. Neither of Nathan's 5K races was particularly fast, but he covered the distance comfortably enough. In my mind I saw him as a beginning distance runner, and so signed him up for the 400 meter and 800 meter events at the track meet, along with some shorter events.

The day was unusually warm for April, sunny with temperatures in the 80s. I advised Nathan to take each race slow, and run at his own pace, regardless of what the other kids were doing. Alas, Nathan had neither the speed, stamina, nor discipline to manage these longer races, and both the 400 and 800 ended in tears and frustration for him. I felt awful.

So I was surprised the following spring when Nathan said that he'd once again like to sign up for track and field. And so here he is, in the pouring rain, focused, determined, even confident, and at the end of the day satisfied with his accomplishments. He is on the cusp of adolescence, and I marvel at how much he has matured. Standing around between events he laughs and jokes easily with the other boys and girls. In each event, regardless of where he finishes, he has a poise that I haven't seen before. He knows what he wants, and he knows the bounds of his capabilities.

In middle school Nathan will sign up for track and field, but ultimately drop it. The full season of meets, and the pressure to compete and achieve, are just not his style.

Born with a sensory processing deficit, Nathan has difficulty responding to multiple sensory stimuli simultaneously. The parallel processing the rest of us do effortlessly, Nathan often has to work through serially. This neurological condition has wide-ranging effects for him. Nathan may never learn to swim. He struggles stepping onto and off of escalators.

Competitive sports that require good eye-hand coordination are difficult for him, as is the cognitive task of being spatially aware of the field of play while understanding the rules, and the tactics of teammates and opposition.

As a solitary activity involving the simplest and most natural of human motions, running has been good for Nathan. Yet later in middle school Nathan will find his true passion. With enough desire and determination, Nathan can overcome his limitations, and he will become passionate about bike riding.

Karen and I had to break the learning process down into many more steps than kids usually require when learning to ride. Nathan started with a tricycle when very young, and then moved to a scooter. A work colleague tipped me off to something called a balance bike, which is a bicycle without pedals.

When Nathan enters middle school we will move him from scooter to balance bike. Finally I will get him a regular bicycle, and try to teach him the final steps to riding. The instinctive tension between father and son intrudes too much, however, and I just can't quite get him there.

In the end, Karen's brother Jeff will be the one to coax Nathan through those final steps of learning to ride. Jeff is a passionate bike rider, and approaches cycling with more of a sense of ethical purpose than anyone I have ever met. He is also a gentler personality than I, and possesses seemingly endless patience. Over the years, Karen and I have relied on Jeff to stay with Nathan so that we can get some couples time away. Jeff shares my love of the outdoors, and his time with Nathan is usually spent outside. They have hiked together, ridden scooters together. And it will be on one of our date outings that Karen will receive a short video clip from Jeff, showing a wobbly but determined Nathan bicycling around the empty parking lot of the elementary school.

By the time Nathan enters high school he will surpass me as a cyclist. That summer we'll do a camping trip up towards Snoqualmie Pass that will feature a hilly, 25 mile loop taking us to Rattlesnake Lake and back. Despite the heat and the hills, Nathan will finish this ride fresh and enthusiastic. I, on the other hand, will be wiped out by the effort.

For my part, my running future is bright. I will complete another marathon, and three more 50Ks. A shift to heart rate training will restore much of the speed that age has taken away. I will turn in my best runs over five years at the Rivalry Run Half Marathon near Lake Sammamish, and at the Wenatchee 10K. I'll have a strong and uplifting race along with 40,000 other runners at the raucous Bloomsday Run in Spokane.

All of this is in the future. Yet it will be this moment, at Nathan's final track meet, to which my thoughts and memories often return. Nathan's hair plastered flat from the rain, glasses covered with droplets, soggy t-shirt clinging to his broad chest, 3rd place ribbon in hand. I gaze at him, and in this ordinary runner I cannot help but admire the extraordinary young man he is starting to become.

OREGON COAST 50K

October 2017 | Yachats, Oregon

Dear 2015 Mark,

This is your future self. I know you're disappointed with dropping out of the Gorge Waterfalls 50k, but I'm here to tell you that it all turns out okay. Let me tell you about the race you just finished, and then about the journey that began with your race.

You've reached the last of the side streets through Yachats, and at the end of the block there's a short tunnel of shrubs that leads back to the wide, grassy bluff where the Adobe Resort overlooks the Pacific Ocean. In front of you, there is not a runner in sight. While you can't see anyone behind you either, you know that Bill and Krissi are close.

Your legs are tired, but as always at the end of a long race it's the ache in your joints that you feel more than anything. The sharp pain in your rib and your left thigh from the fall you took aren't helping any either. Something is going on there; time to think about that later.

Truly the pain and fatigue feel distant, like they are happening to someone else. You find that you're no longer just plodding along, but have picked it up to a brisk jog. The ocean on your left, the town on your right, the sound of the surf in your ear, you continue to increase your tempo to a run.

You often dream of running. In those dreams you are weightless, touching only lightly on the ground, and every stride feels effortless. You do not run so much as flow. Flow. You are in it now, as if you were in a dream.

How long now? A half mile? The day hikers and locals are clapping and cheering, and in the distance you can hear the sound of cowbells. You smile. Only a runner can really appreciate the joy of hearing cowbells. The cheers carry you along, and as you round the corner of the Resort you can see the finish line. Standing just on the other side, Rainshadow Running's race director James Varner waits, as he always does, to personally greet every runner who crosses. You're sprinting now; you don't even know how, but you're sprinting. You can feel the wide grin on your face, and in a last burst you're across the finish line and James and you are high fiving. You sneak a quick glance at the clock, and it shows 7 hours 39 minutes; under the cutoff time by 21 minutes.

You step away from the finish line, and walk out of the corral. Looking back you still don't see another runner, but you can hear the cheers of the crowd from around the corner of the Resort. It's Bill, coming into sight and chugging up that last slope to the finish line. You clap and hoot and holler with the rest as he and James embrace in a bear hug. Looking over James's shoulder, Bill catches your eye and gives you a smile.

The crowd is cheering again, and sure enough it's Krissi. Spent, but determined, she runs it in across the finish line. After she crosses, she sees you clapping, and nods. As she comes out of the corral, you congratulate her. "Well done, girl."

She smiles a now familiar smile. "Thanks, you too."

And with that, the moment is over. The pain and fatigue begin to wash over you. There is food — so much food — awaiting, and cold beer in the beer garden, and you're looking for your friend Greg who volunteered this day, and you want to let Karen know that you're okay.

31 miles. 4500 feet of elevation gain. Your third 50k completed, and the outcome never in doubt. That's right, 2015 Mark. From that tough moment just down the trail from Multnomah Falls until here, from that necessary but disappointing decision to drop, you have completed not one but three 50k races.

Of course there was Defiance 50K in Tacoma later that year. Then last year you took on a more ambitious 50k at Baker Lake. Over 4000 feet of elevation gain, no single big climb, but lots of unrelenting ups and downs accompanied by rugged single track of roots, granite, and damp, moss-covered footbridges over the many streams and gullies. You finished, despite digging deeper than you expected down the last few miles.

But there's no race quite like a Rainshadow Running event — a joyous finish area celebration, well organized with great volunteers, but tough, sometimes to the point of cruelty. Know what you're doing, and train carefully, when you sign up for one a Rainshadow event.

Some Rainshadow events you won't even try. Yakima Ridge, with an abundance of elevation gain and no shade or cover from the Central Washington summer sun. No. Orcas Island, in January, with over 8000 feet of elevation gain guaranteed to be cold, slippery, and muddy since that is the heart of the rainy season on the San Juan Islands. Again, no.

Winthrop Marathon just about did you in, with the final eight miles of summer sun turning an apparent PR into an epic struggle you weren't sure you'd finish. And Gorge Waterfalls, with its 6000 feet of elevation gain, including a final climb of 2400 feet (where you flamed out), was arrogance to the point of hubris as a first attempt at a 50k. You know that now.

Still, you had unfinished business with Rainshadow Running. Finish a Rainshadow ultra, and finish it under control, and you know you really belong in the ultra community. And so, 2015 Mark, you found yourself at the start of the Oregon Coast 50k, seeking redemption.

From the town of Yachats, the 250 runners are bused north to a state park beach. The course then takes you down the beach for six miles back to Yachats and the first checkpoint. You've done a bit of beach running, and you know how deceptively sand can sap stamina out of you. So you have a game plan. Slow jog for two minutes, then walk for one minute. Repeat, until you clear the beach.

James sounds the start, and runners take off. You start with a minute of walking, and then begin your slow jog. By then you can barely see the rest of the runners, carried away by their enthusiasm, and lost in the morning fog.

By Mile 2 you are alone, so far back that you can't even see another runner. You start to doubt your strategy. Are you taking this section too slow? Should you be banking more time for later sections of the course? Why has everyone else surged so far ahead? You stick to your plan. Around Mile 4 you pass one runner, and as you head off the beach and into Yachats you pass another. Then you're through the first checkpoint. It's 10:20; you're almost an hour ahead of the cutoff time.

The next several miles are flat as the course works its way through town and then down Highway 101 a bit. You follow the course markers off the highway and onto dirt single track that plunges into the forest. Almost immediately the trail turns into a steep, switchback upgrade.

You've trained and planned for this. It's about a 900 foot climb, and though it feels oppressive, even stifling with the dense foliage and high humidity, you're confident. Mostly you keep it to a brisk walk, but any reasonably flat stretch, even just 20 or 30 feet, you pick up to an easy jog.

Now you're picking off runners one after another — all those who set off too fast on the sand and didn't conserve enough energy for the uphills. You reach a level stretch after about 600 feet of climbing, and you've passed ten runners at this point.

The group you're in the middle of is somewhere around Mile 11 at this point, and in front of you is a young woman with sandy blonde hair, freckles, and a big smile. Her name is Krissi, she's from Las Vegas, and this is her first 50k. You play leap frog for a bit, and then on the next upgrade you pass her. She calls out, "You're an inspiration; you motivate me!"

You puzzle over this statement for the remainder of the race. Why? Because I'm old? You're slightly annoyed by that. Not annoyed by her; she's a ray of sunshine. But offended at the idea that age could be a barrier.

When you turned 50 you had never run more than seven miles. Now you're 57 and you've completed two 50ks, four marathons, and more half marathons than you can count.

Runners. We grab motivation wherever we can. Just like Krissi.

Finally you top out the big hill, and are rewarded with a spectacular panorama view of the Oregon Coast. The view is worth every step of the climb it took to get there.

"Now that's a view worth fighting for," says a runner ahead of you who has paused to take a picture.

You begin the steep switchbacks downhill, pushing to the back of your mind that you will have to climb this same grade in a matter of hours. Careening down the hill, hopping over roots and rocks, you barrel past another ten runners.

It happens in an instant — so fast that you're laid out on the ground before you can react. You pivot on a hairpin turn around a boulder, and as you're coming out of the bottom of the turn your left foot snags a root. Crumbling to your left you slam into the boulder with your chest and thigh taking the impact. You hit so hard that you bounce off the boulder and crash down on the trail on your right side, skidding to a halt with your right calf grinding on the trail. Shakily you get up, brush yourself off, and, in that tunnel vision mindset that runners know so well, resume your full tilt descent.

In the weeks ahead, unable to do a situp, it will dawn on you that you may have cracked a rib. It will also take weeks for the bruising on your left thigh to subside, and the gash on your right calf to heal. In the moment, the episode is already forgotten.

At the bottom of the switchbacks is Checkpoint 2, and you power through, 45 minutes ahead of the cutoff time. The next cutoff time will be at this same aid station, ten miles from now. As you're heading out Krissi bounds in. "How are you doing?"

"Not bad," you say. "I only fell once."

She nods. "Didn't see it, but I heard it."

The next two miles offer easy, rolling single track. You catch up to a guy named Bill who looks to be about your age. Looks can be deceiving; you will learn later that Bill is 69. Bill seems to be something of a fixture in the local trail running community. Many of the runners you encounter greet him by name. He has powerful calves that you are envious of, but runs with a noticeable limp. Not a big deal; you've been told that you run with a limp.

After a couple of miles the trail turns uphill again. This climb is not as steep as the previous climb but is more sustained. For the next four miles there are no level or downhill breaks; the only variance is the steepness of the climb. You are gaining 1500 feet over this stretch, meaning the average grade over this section is 7%. Bill and his monster calf muscles leave you well behind at this point.

You pass a few runners, but several runners pass you as well. Most people are power walking; there is very little running on this stretch. It takes you almost two hours to make this ascent, and it feels brutally unrelenting. You saw a runner literally reduced to tears over the effort required. Again, runners are paying the price for having left too much energy in the sand on the beach. You keep waiting for the unsteady, rubber-legged feeling that will signal that you're spent. You remember that feeling well from your collapse at Gorges Waterfalls 50k, but it never comes.

An athlete's flow comes from those moments when they summon their full capability, often without realizing it, and they are no longer fighting the challenge but flowing with it. Gradually it dawns on you that you are in the flow. Your legs keep powering you on. You push away thought of the big steep climb awaiting you beyond the last checkpoint. Your entire focus is to make the last cutoff time, and leave whatever stamina you have on the trail after that.

You come upon two women runners, one administering first aid to the other.

She calls out, "Watch the stump in the middle there. There's a wasp nest in the base of it." Duly warned, you skirt by without incident. The challenges of trail running are many, and varied.

At last you reach the aid station at the top of the ridge. Every aid station has been fantastic, with a volunteer at the ready asking, "What do you need?" Water bottles are quickly refilled, and the fueling choices are abundant, from fruit to chips to sandwiches, nuts or candy. You're in and out in less than five minutes, doubling back the way you have just come.

Moments out of the aid station, you see Krissi on the way in. Her big grin is gone, drained away by the long climb. When she sees you she manages a quick smile. "We got this," you call out, and you part.

You're a little worried about the cutoff time, with only an hour to go to get back to the last checkpoint. But the return route forks off the trail you ascended, following a shorter and smoother trail back down the ridge. Also, no hornets.

You're about halfway down the descent when Krissi catches up to you, smiling once again and obviously happy to be enjoying some downhill running. You run together for a bit, chatting as you go. The trail makes a brief upturn for about a quarter mile.

"What the heck?"

"I know, this wasn't in the guide book."

"I'm definitely asking my travel agent for a refund."

You both top out this stretch and return to steady downhill. Krissi looks relieved, and says, "I'm such a weenie on the uphills." Don't worry about it Krissi; we all are.

At that moment a big step down jars your water bottle loose from your belt. You stop to pick it up. With an impish grin, Krissi flashes by, calling out, "See ya!"

You roll your eyes, but by the time you have situated everything and resume running, she is out of sight.

A short while later you roll into the final aid station, and seconds behind you Bill comes in. One of the volunteers says to you, "You guys are doing great. Half an hour ahead of the cutoff time. You're going to finish this thing."

They get your water bottles filled, and turn to Bill's. He scans the table and says, "Oh man, is that pickle juice? Pour some of that right in there."

The volunteer looks at him questioningly, and Bill waves him on. In goes the pickle juice. Bill then adds a powder he's been carrying, and the entire concoction immediately turns black.

The wide-eyed volunteer asks, "What is that stuff?"

A twinkle in his eye, Bill says, "I'd take the time to tell you, but if I don't drink this quick it'll eat right through the bottle."

With that Bill heads up the trail, and you follow. Behind you the two volunteers are roaring with laughter.

"I love ultra runners, man. You guys are the best. You're crazy!"

And here you are. Seven miles to go, but really it's the 1000 feet of elevation gain over the next two miles that stands between you and the finish line. You know at this point that you're going to finish. You don't know if you're going to make the 5:00 PM finish line cutoff time. Bill quickly outpaces you on the ascent, and no one is anywhere close behind. You are alone on the trail, just you and one last big climb.

Power walking your way up, you really have no idea what you have left in the tank at this point. You are waiting for that empty, spent feeling that comes in the closing miles of every marathon and ultra you have run. One switchback. Then another. And another. On and on. Then suddenly you're at the overlook, and the Oregon coast panorama is spread out before you once again.
The spent feeling never comes. You know the next mile or so is level and

then you have another 300 feet or so of climb to do, but your confidence soars. You're going to finish. And you are going to hit the 5:00 PM cutoff time.

At last you top out the climb, and fly down the steep downhill. Near the bottom you catch up to Bill. He waves you past, but you pull back, saying, "No, you're setting a good pace." You chat a bit, but his words get shorter and his breathing is labored. You realize that he is holding you back and you slip by him.

The trail bottoms out to a short, rolling section that will put you back on Highway 101. You're in full tunnel vision mode now, and as you pass another runner it takes you a moment to realize it's Krissi. She too is struggling; that last climb obviously took a lot out of her. You slow down and give her some encouragement. She manages a smile that's more of a grimace, but she's game. For the next mile or so she keeps pace with you.

You come to Highway 101, and a volunteer holds you up for a moment so that traffic can pass. Another runner joins you waiting. It's Bill. Then the three of you cross the highway, and turn towards Yachats, the town now in sight. You are surprised to feel like you have some reserve left, so you pick up the pace. As you enter town, you look over your shoulder and see Bill, about a 100 yards behind. About 50 yards behind him is Krissi, not running fast but definitely running and not walking.

The onlookers clap and cheer, and now you can hear the sound of the surf off to your left. You look back again at them and smile. The finish line awaits.

So, 2015 Mark, what have you learned in the intervening years? First of all, your future selves owe you a lot. In dropping out of Gorge Waterfalls 50k you confronted failure, but chose not to see it as defeat. You have steadily built on lessons learned, starting with the first and most important: "The only way to learn how to run a 50k is to run a 50k."

Hard as it is to confront, let's recap what went wrong that day so I can show you how you've grown:

- You over-trained and under-prepared — too many training miles run at too high an intensity, and not enough mental preparation.

- You chased cutoff times instead of letting the race flow to you — again, poor mental preparation.

- You started too fast, ran too hard through the middle miles, and had no measure of what your overall exertion level was.

- Poor fueling. It was almost Mile 10 before you slowed down for your first water or fuel, and that's too late in the race for hasty consumption through the middle stretch to catch you up.

- For a runner, you were overweight. At 6'5" your ideal running weight should be closer to 190 than 210.

Since then you have tackled these challenges thoughtfully and analytically (note that these are not the same thing). You have been patient. And you have made steady progress.

- You have read from people wiser than you. "Meb for Mortals" has a lot of great information, but his attention to the particular needs of older runners was a revelation. No book has impacted you as much as "Primal Fitness", teaching you the value of rest, the value of running by feel, and the importance of running slow to build a base from which to run faster.

- You have taken up heart rate training and stuck consistently to it for almost two years now. More than anything heart rate monitoring has given you a measure of level of effort that clues you in when you are pushing too hard. You have broken out of the "no pain no gain" cycle, and are healthier than you have been in a long time.

- You've recognized low carb eating as an essential companion to heart rate training and the holistic effort to reset your metabolism from carb burning to fat burning. As a result, you stepped up to the starting line at Oregon Coast 50k, 17 pounds lighter than you had been at the start of Baker Lake 50k a year earlier.

- You've taken weight training and other cross training exercises seriously. While this aspect of staying fit has always been, and still is a chore for you mentally, you've pursued it with discipline. You have more power and flexibility now than you had at the start of Gorge Waterfalls 50k.

- You have listened to your friends, and learned from their experiences and advice. For example, Endurolyte has proven to be a key to electrolyte balance on a low carb fueling strategy.

- You have made the wilderness your religion, and running the high alpine trails of Mount Rainier your church. There you have found kindred spirits who have shared their trail lore with you and welcomed you as one of their own. And you have found the calm and patience to let the trail flow to you.

There is so much still to learn. Indeed, this blend of intellectual and physical challenge is an essential part of what appeals to you about running. But know this: you made a choice to be humble yet positive, to grow and learn from failure, and we, your future selves, will honor that choice. We will pass that torch to future selves yet to come, and of course we will pass that torch to Nathan.

So it is with happiness and gratitude that I lay your ghost to rest, redeemed at last. You now belong to that small community of Pacific Northwest trail runners who have crossed the finish line of a Rainshadow Running ultra with confidence and control.

RUNNING MOUNT RAINIER IN PICTURES

- **Evans Creek Run** (https://photos.app.goo.gl/1LtjRqhjxrjuiyEd9)
- **Spring Approach to Mowich Lake**
  (https://photos.app.goo.gl/ZASuAPqwqAhnDYV58)
- **Carbon River Run** (https://photos.app.goo.gl/oWtnL4ce4F74gD5y7)
- **The Loop** (https://photos.app.goo.gl/gy3qs4tq9afXc1Bd8)
- **Moraine Park Run** (https://photos.app.goo.gl/9oQuvH4XnnhpbdPJ7)
- **Echo Lake Run** (https://photos.app.goo.gl/nJ1AiuHJDuyciW5F8)
- **Sunrise > Grand Park > Lake Eleanor**
  (https://photos.app.goo.gl/TYLu112eHE44sJAB8)
- **Palisades Trail** (https://photos.app.goo.gl/fpm9LCBuor7m3qLE9)
- **Windy Gap Run** (https://photos.app.goo.gl/1pj7viDCSg4MMi199)
- **Green Lake Run** (https://photos.app.goo.gl/zV155kWHnNnM9uYZ8)
- **Ranger Falls** (https://photos.app.goo.gl/1J3XZpn4rrdMup68A)
- **Carbon Glacier Run** (https://photos.app.goo.gl/F3DbBjJtugRjkuLB9)
- **Mowich River Run** (https://photos.app.goo.gl/Fpy4LTZZiEQ8nbK06)
- **Skookum Falls Run** (https://photos.app.goo.gl/bkN13uHr95etVS016)

www.ingramcontent.com/pod-product-compliance
Lightning Source LLC
Chambersburg PA
CBHW051516030726

47592CB00006B/2299